ACCELERATING CIRCULAR ECONOMY USING DIGITAL TRANSFORMATION

Circular Economy using Digital Transformation

VIJAY KARNA, PHD

INDIA • SINGAPORE • MALAYSIA

Contents

Acknowledgments

The creation of a book is a collaborative endeavor that draws upon the contributions and support of many individuals and organizations. "Accelerating Circular Economy Using Digital Transformation" is no exception, and I extend our heartfelt gratitude to those who have been instrumental in bringing this project to fruition.

First and foremost, I express my sincere appreciation to my family and loved ones for their unwavering support and understanding during the long hours and late nights dedicated to research and writing. Your encouragement has been the foundation of our perseverance.

I am deeply indebted to the experts and professionals who graciously shared their knowledge and insights, enriching the content of this book. Your willingness to collaborate and your passion for the circular economy and digital transformation have been a constant source of inspiration.

My appreciation goes out to my colleagues and friends who offered valuable feedback, advice, and encouragement throughout the book's development. Your diverse perspectives and expertise have greatly contributed to the book's depth and quality.

I would like to extend our gratitude to the reviewers and editors who painstakingly reviewed the manuscript, providing constructive criticism and recommendations to enhance the book's clarity and accuracy.

The support of the publishing team at Notion Press has been instrumental in bringing this book to life. We thank them for their professionalism, guidance, and commitment to making this project a success.

Furthermore, I acknowledge the countless organizations and individuals working tirelessly to advance the circular economy and digital transformation. Your dedication to sustainability and innovation serves as the driving force behind the ideas presented in this book.

Finally, I thank my readers for their interest in this important subject matter. We hope that the insights and knowledge shared in this book will inspire and empower you to contribute to the acceleration of the circular economy using digital transformation.

This book is a testament to the power of collaboration and the collective pursuit of a more sustainable and prosperous future. I am truly grateful for the support and contributions of everyone involved in this project.

With heartfelt thanks,
Vijay Karna

Preface

Welcome to "Accelerating Circular Economy Using Digital Transformation." This book explores the transformative potential of digital technologies in advancing the circular economy, a concept poised to revolutionize the way we produce, consume, and manage resources. As we embark on this journey, let us take a moment to set the stage for what lies ahead.

I. Introduction

1. **The Concept of the Circular Economy**: The circular economy is an innovative approach aimed at minimizing waste, maximizing resource efficiency, and fundamentally reshaping our industrial and consumption processes.

2. **The Role of Digital Transformation in Accelerating the Circular Economy**: We will examine how digital technologies, ranging from IoT and AI to blockchain, can act as accelerators, driving the transition towards circular practices.

3. **The Purpose and Scope of the Book**: This section provides an overview of the book's goals and structure, helping you navigate the chapters that follow.

II. The Circular Economy

1. **Overview of the Circular Economy and its Benefits**: Delve into the fundamentals of the circular economy and discover the myriad benefits it offers for sustainability, business, and society.

2. **Case Studies of Circular Economy Models**: Real-world examples of organizations and industries successfully implementing circular economy practices will illuminate the possibilities and challenges.

3. **Challenges in Implementing Circular Economy Practices**: We explore the barriers and hurdles that can hinder the transition to a circular economy and discuss strategies for overcoming them.

4. **Link between Circular Economy & UN SDGs**: Understand the critical connection between the circular economy and the United Nations Sustainable Development Goals.

III. Digital Transformation

1. **Overview of Digital Transformation and its Benefits**: Uncover the essence of digital transformation, its impact on various sectors, and the opportunities it presents.

2. **Case Studies of Digital Transformation in Different Industries**: Explore how diverse industries have harnessed digital technologies to innovate, optimize, and transform their operations.

3. **Challenges in Implementing Digital Transformation**: We confront the challenges that organizations face when embarking on digital transformation journeys and offer insights into mitigation strategies.

IV. Intersection of Circular Economy and Digital Transformation

1. **Opportunities for Using Digital Technologies to Accelerate the Circular Economy**: Discover the synergies between the circular economy and digital transformation, and the potential for digital tools to enhance circular practices.
2. **Examples of Successful Circular Economy Practices Enhanced by Digital Transformation**: This section provides compelling instances of how digital technologies have supercharged circular business models.
3. **Challenges Faced While Using Digital Technology for Circular Economy**: Recognize and address the hurdles and complexities that emerge when marrying digital transformation with circularity.

V. Assessment of Circular Business Models

1. **Circular Supply Model Assessment Using Digital Transformation**: Learn how to assess the effectiveness of circular supply chain models enhanced by digital tools.
2. **Resource Recovery Model Assessment**: Explore the evaluation of resource recovery strategies within a circular context.
3. **Product Life Extension Model Assessment**: Understand how to measure the success of strategies aimed at extending the life of products.
4. **Sharing Model Assessment**: Assess the impact and feasibility of sharing economy models within the circular economy.
5. **Product Service System Model Assessment**: Examine the assessment criteria for product service systems in the circular economy.

VI. Building the Circular Economy with Digital Transformation

1. **Steps to Implement a Circular Economy Model with Digital Technologies**: Follow a practical guide on initiating and sustaining circular practices using digital tools.

2. **Case Studies of Successful Circular Economy Models Built with Digital Transformation**: Explore real-world success stories and gain insights into the strategies employed.

3. **The Role of Government Policies and Regulations in Accelerating Circular Economy Through Digital Transformation**: Recognize the importance of policy frameworks in promoting circular practices.

VII. Challenges and Solutions

1. **Common Challenges in Implementing Circular Economy Models with Digital Transformation**: Identify recurring obstacles and their root causes.

2. **Solutions to Overcome These Challenges**: Discover potential solutions and mitigation strategies to address these challenges.

3. **Implementation of Solutions**: Understand the practical steps to implement solutions in real-world contexts.

VIII. Relation Between Circular Economics and Life Cycle Assessment

1. **Strengths of Life Cycle Assessment to Assess Circular Economy Strategies**: Explore the use of Life Cycle Assessment (LCA) as a tool for evaluating circular economy strategies.

2. **Challenges of Applying LCA to Assess Circular Economy Strategies**: Recognize the limitations and complexities of applying LCA to circular practices.

3. **Advantages and Recommendations of the Life Cycle Initiative with Case Studies**: Discover how initiatives such as the Life Cycle Initiative can enhance circularity assessment, supported by relevant case studies.

IX. Circularity Assessment Tool

This section introduces a practical tool for assessing the circularity of products, processes, or organizations.

X. Conclusion

1. **Summary of Key Points**: We recap the essential takeaways from each chapter.

2. **Future Outlook for the Intersection of Circular Economy and Digital Transformation**: We peer into the horizon, envisioning the evolving landscape of circular practices empowered by digital transformation.

Our journey through the intersection of the circular economy and digital transformation is just beginning. Together, we will explore how these transformative concepts can reshape our world, unlocking sustainable and efficient solutions to some of our most pressing challenges. Let's embark on this exciting journey of discovery and innovation.

Happy reading!

01

Introduction

The world is facing a growing number of environmental challenges such as climate change, depletion of natural resources, and waste generation. These issues have highlighted the need for a more sustainable approach to economic development, one that reduces waste and resource consumption while also creating economic value. One solution that has gained significant attention is the circular economy, which focuses on creating a closed-loop system where resources are kept in use for as long as possible, extracting maximum value from them, and minimizing waste and pollution.

Digital technologies have the potential to accelerate the transition towards circular economy by facilitating the sharing and management of information, improving the efficiency of resource use, and enabling new business models. In this book, we will explore how digital transformation can be used to accelerate the adoption of circular economy principles across different industries and sectors.

The book will start by introducing the concept of circular economy and why it is important for creating a sustainable future. We will then discuss the different ways digital transformation can support the circular economy, such as IoT, big data, and blockchain. We will also explore how digital technologies can be used to support circular design and product development, enabling the creation of products that are more easily disassembled and recycled.

Furthermore, we will discuss how circular supply chains can be created using digital technologies, and how they can help reduce waste and resource consumption while also creating economic value. We will explore different circular business models that can be implemented using digital technologies, such as product-as-a-service and circular leasing. We will also provide case studies of organizations that have successfully implemented circular economy strategies using digital technologies, helping readers understand the practical application of the concepts discussed in the book.

Finally, we will discuss the role of policy and regulatory frameworks in supporting circular economy and digital transformation. We will highlight the policies and regulations that can help accelerate the transition towards a circular economy, and how digital technologies can be used to support the implementation of these policies.

This book is intended for anyone interested in sustainability, circular economy, and digital transformation. It is particularly relevant for business leaders, policymakers, and entrepreneurs looking to create more sustainable and circular business models. By exploring the intersection of digital transformation and circular economy, we hope to inspire new ideas and strategies for accelerating the transition towards a more sustainable future.

1.1 The concept of the circular economy

Circular economy is an alternative model of economic development that aims to reduce waste, conserve resources, and create a sustainable future. It is a system that aims to keep resources in use for as long as possible, extracting the maximum value from them before recovering and regenerating them. This approach is in stark contrast to the traditional linear economy, where products are produced, used, and then disposed of as waste. The concept of circular economy is gaining momentum worldwide, as organizations and governments recognize the urgent need to transition towards a more sustainable and resilient economy.

The traditional linear economy model of take-make-dispose has resulted in unsustainable resource consumption and environmental degradation. In contrast, the circular economy aims to decouple economic growth from resource consumption by promoting closed-loop systems where waste is minimized and resources are conserved through reuse, repair, and recycling. This chapter provides an overview of the concept of the circular economy, its principles, benefits, and challenges.

The concept of circular economy is a relatively new economic model that has gained attention in recent years as an alternative to the traditional linear economy. In a linear economy, resources are extracted, products are made, used and then discarded as waste. In contrast, in a circular economy, waste is minimized, resources are conserved, and products are designed for reuse and recycling. We will explore the concept of circular economy, its principles, and its benefits.

Illustration of a Circualr Economy by Design

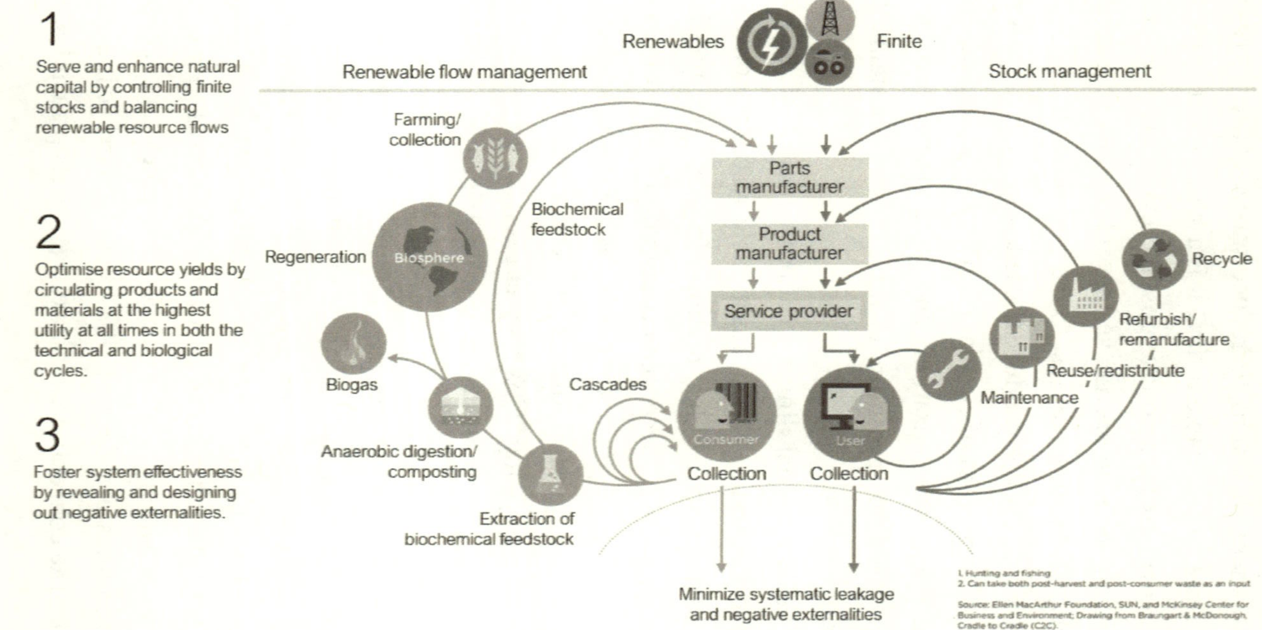

The circular economy butterfly
The butterfly center

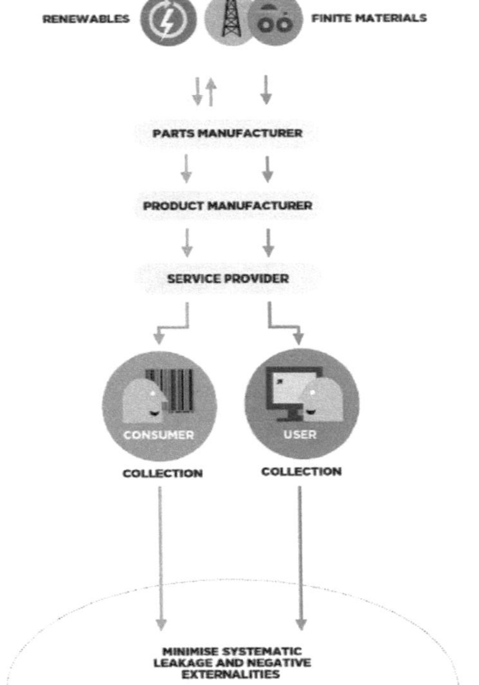

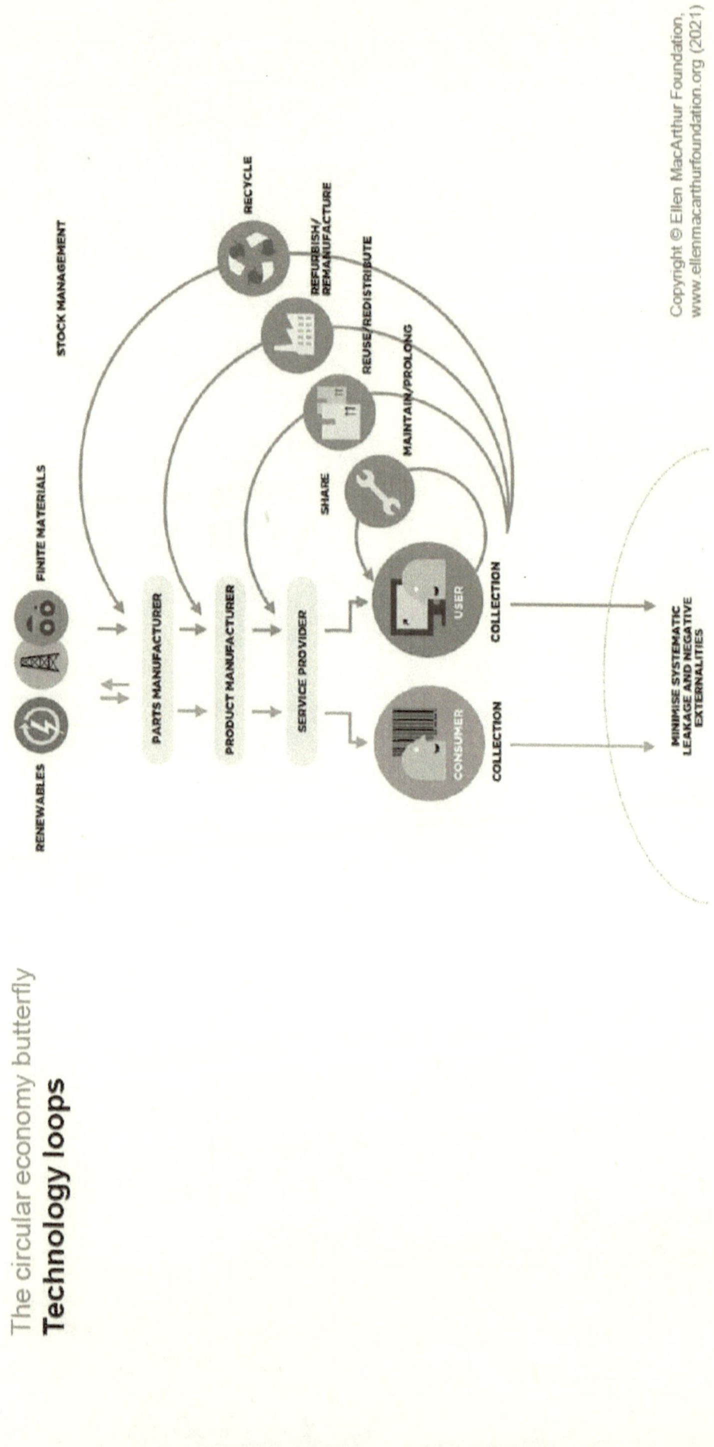
The circular economy butterfly
Technology loops
RENEWABLES
FINITE MATERIALS
STOCK MANAGEMENT
PARTS MANUFACTURER
PRODUCT MANUFACTURER
SERVICE PROVIDER
CONSUMER
USER
SHARE
MAINTAIN/PROLONG
REUSE/REDISTRIBUTE
REFURBISH/
REMANUFACTURE
RECYCLE
COLLECTION
COLLECTION
MINIMISE SYSTEMATIC
LEAKAGE AND NEGATIVE
EXTERNALITIES
Copyright © Ellen MacArthur Foundation,
www.ellenmacarthurfoundation.org (2021)

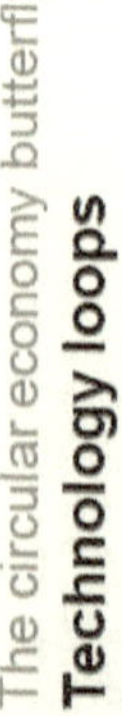

The circular economy butterfly
Biological loops

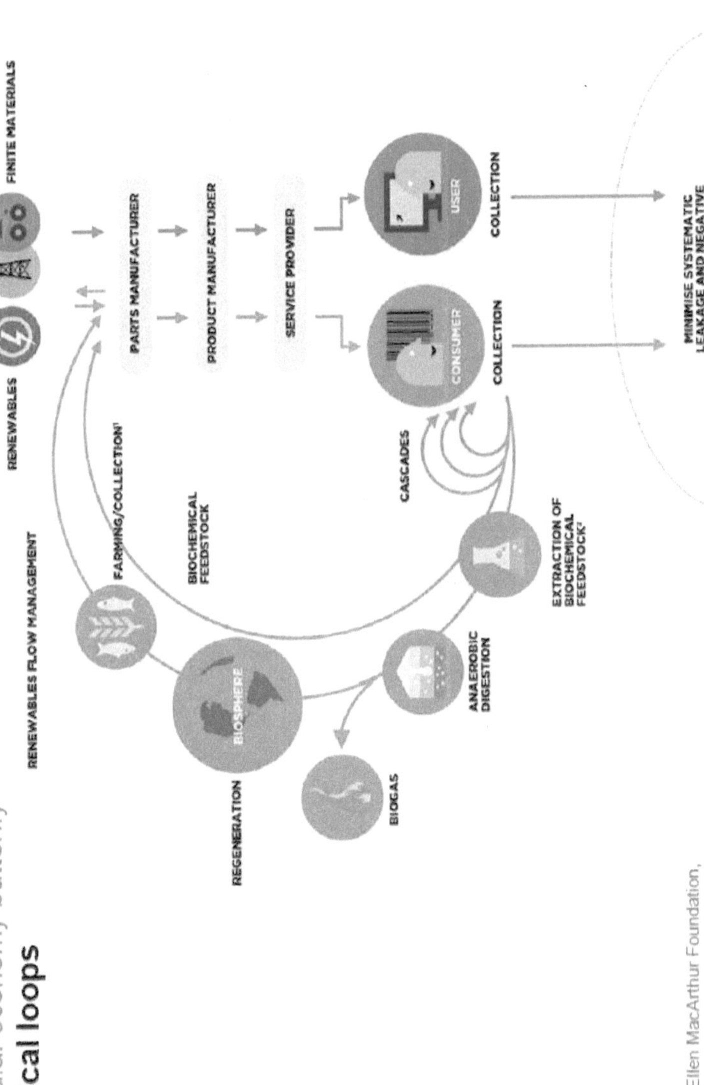

The circular economy butterfly
Learning points

- The Ellen MacArthur Foundation has produced a well-known graphical representation of the circular economy known as the "butterfly diagram".

- The central component shows how design, materials, and energy add value at various stages.

- The right wing shows how various feedback loops can be used to retain and enhance value for **technical** materials and products.

- The left wing illustrates how **biological** materials can be reused and cascaded until they are returned to the natural in such a way as to enhance and regenerate the biosphere.

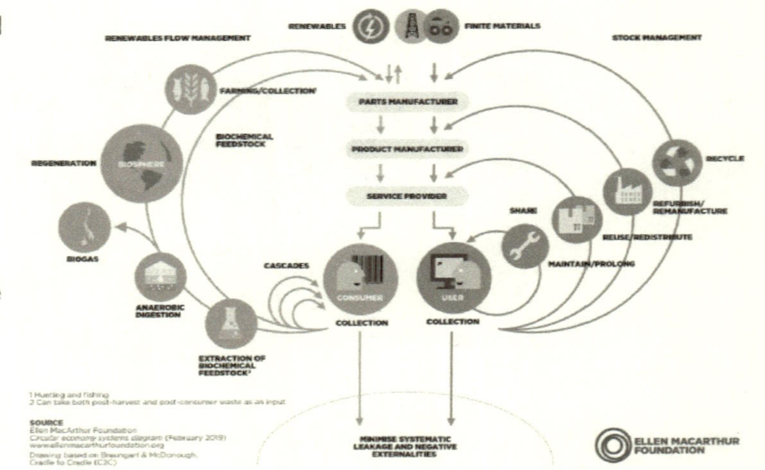

Principles of Circular Economy:

The circular economy is based on three core principles: design out waste and pollution, keep products and materials in use, and regenerate natural systems. These principles are interdependent and interconnected and are underpinned by the concept of a circular value chain that encompasses every stage of the product lifecycle, from design to disposal.

a. **Design out Waste and Pollution:** The first principle of the circular economy is to design out waste and pollution by rethinking the way products are made and used. This involves designing products that can be easily disassembled, repaired, and upgraded, and avoiding the use of toxic materials and chemicals. It also involves designing products that are durable, efficient, and easy to recycle, thus reducing the amount of waste generated at the end of the product lifecycle.

b. **Keep Products and Materials in Use:** The second principle of the circular economy is to keep products and materials in use for as long as possible. This involves creating closed-loop systems where products and materials are reused, repaired, and recycled, rather than disposed of as waste. It also involves creating new business models, such as product-as-a-service and circular leasing, that incentivize companies to maintain and reuse their products rather than selling them as disposable goods.

c. **Regenerate Natural Systems:** The third principle of the circular economy is to regenerate natural systems by restoring and preserving the environment. This involves promoting sustainable resource use and reducing the carbon footprint of production and consumption. It also involves restoring ecosystems, protecting biodiversity, and promoting renewable energy and resource-efficient technologies.

Benefits of Circular Economy:

The circular economy offers several benefits, including:

Reduced Resource Consumption: The circular economy reduces the use of finite resources by promoting closed-loop systems where waste is minimized, and resources are conserved through reuse and recycling.

a. **Cost Savings:** The circular economy promotes resource efficiency and reduces waste, leading to cost savings for businesses and individuals.

b. **Job Creation:** The circular economy creates new jobs in areas such as product design, repair, and recycling.

c. **Reduced Environmental Impact:** The circular economy reduces environmental impact by promoting sustainable resource use, reducing pollution, and restoring ecosystems.

d. **Increased Resilience:** The circular economy promotes resilience by reducing dependence on finite resources and reducing exposure to resource price volatility.

Challenges of Circular Economy:

The circular economy faces several challenges, including:

a. **Complex Value Chains:** The circular economy requires coordination and collaboration across the entire value chain, from product design to disposal, which can be complex and challenging.

b. **Inconsistent Regulations:** Regulations and policies around circular economy are inconsistent across regions and countries, which can hinder the development of circular economy initiatives.

c. **Limited Infrastructure:** The circular economy requires infrastructure for waste management, recycling, and reuse, which can be limited in some regions.

d. **Behavioral Change:** The circular economy requires a shift in consumer behavior towards more sustainable and circular consumption patterns, which can be difficult to achieve.

e. **Cultural Barriers:** The circular economy requires a cultural shift towards valuing sustainable resource use, reducing waste, and preserving the environment, which can be challenging to achieve.

The circular economy offers a promising approach to address the challenges of unsustainable resource consumption and environmental degradation. The circular economy's principles of designing out waste and pollution, keeping products and materials in use, and regenerating natural systems offer a framework for promoting sustainable resource use and reducing waste. The circular economy faces several challenges, including complex value chains.

1.2 The role of digital transformation in accelerating the circular economy

Digital transformation is transforming the way we live and work, and it has the potential to accelerate the transition towards a circular economy. By leveraging digital technologies, businesses can improve resource efficiency, optimize supply chains, and reduce waste. This article will explore the role of digital transformation in accelerating the circular economy, its benefits, and its challenges.

Digital Technologies for Circular Economy:

Digital technologies can play a critical role in accelerating the circular economy in several ways:

a. **Internet of Things (IoT):** IoT sensors can track and monitor products and materials throughout the product lifecycle, enabling better management of resources and waste.

b. **Big Data Analytics:** Big data analytics can help businesses analyze and optimize supply chains, reducing waste and improving resource efficiency.

c. **Artificial Intelligence (AI):** AI can help businesses predict and prevent waste, optimize resource use, and enable better decision-making.

d. **Blockchain:** Blockchain can improve supply chain transparency and traceability, enabling better management of resources and waste.

Benefits of Digital Transformation for Circular Economy:

Digital transformation offers several benefits for accelerating the circular economy:

a. **Resource efficiency:** Digital technologies can help businesses optimize resource use, reducing waste and improving resource productivity.

b.   **Supply chain optimization:** Digital technologies can improve supply chain transparency and traceability, enabling better management of resources and waste.

c.   **Innovation:** Digital technologies can enable new business models and circular products, accelerating the transition towards a circular economy.

d.   **Collaboration:** Digital technologies can enable collaboration among businesses, governments, and consumers, driving the transition towards a circular economy.

Challenges and Limitations:

While digital transformation offers several benefits for accelerating the circular economy, there are also challenges and limitations that need to be addressed:

a.   **Investment:** Implementing digital transformation requires significant investment in technology, infrastructure, and skills.

b.   **Adoption:** Many businesses may be resistant to change and slow to adopt digital technologies.

c.   **Data privacy and security:** Digital transformation raises concerns about data privacy and security, which need to be addressed to ensure trust and adoption.

d.   **Infrastructure:** Digital transformation requires reliable and robust infrastructure to support its implementation, which may not be available in all regions.

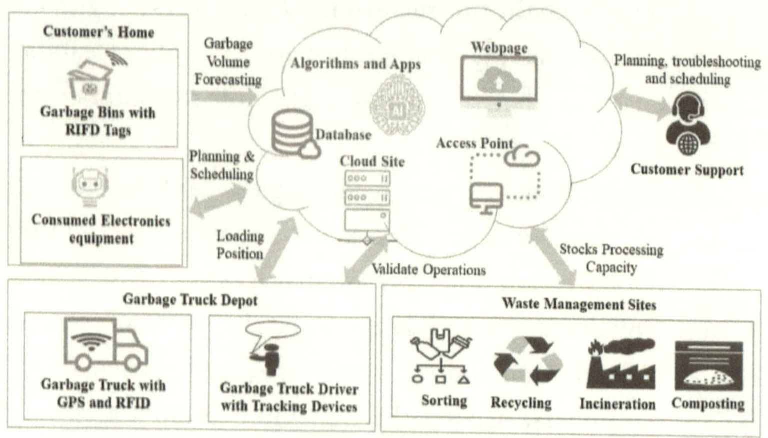

Image source: https://www.sciencedirect.com/science/article/abs/pii/S0959652622015219

Case Studies:

Several businesses have successfully leveraged digital transformation to accelerate the transition towards a circular economy:

a.   **Philips:** Philips has developed circular products such as lighting-as-a-service, which uses IoT sensors to monitor lighting usage and optimize energy efficiency.

b.   **H&M:** H&M has developed a circular business model where customers can return used clothes, which are then recycled into new products.

c.   **Cisco:** Cisco has developed circular supply chains, using blockchain to improve supply chain transparency and traceability.

d.   **Interface:** Interface has developed circular carpet tiles, using recycled materials and designing for end-of-life reuse and recycling.

Digital transformation offers significant potential to accelerate the transition towards a circular economy. By leveraging digital technologies, businesses can improve resource efficiency, optimize supply chains, and reduce waste. However, implementing digital transformation requires significant investment and may face challenges related to adoption, data privacy and security, and infrastructure. Despite these challenges, several businesses have successfully implemented digital transformation to accelerate the circular economy, demonstrating the potential benefits of this approach. The role of digital transformation in accelerating the circular economy is likely to become increasingly important in the coming years as businesses and governments look to transition towards a more sustainable economic model.

1.3 The purpose and scope of the book

The purpose of this book is to provide readers with a comprehensive understanding of how digital transformation can be used to accelerate the transition to a circular economy. It explores the integration of digital technologies and circular economy practices to create a more sustainable and efficient economy that reduces waste, improves resource efficiency, and increases economic value.

The book's scope covers a range of topics related to circular economy and digital transformation. It provides an overview of circular economy principles and the benefits it offers over the traditional linear economy. It also examines digital transformation technologies, including blockchain, artificial intelligence, the internet of things, and machine learning, and their potential applications to circular economy practices.

The book further discusses how digital transformation can facilitate circular economy practices, and how these practices can contribute to the achievement of sustainable development goals. It explores the integration of digital technologies into various sectors such as manufacturing, logistics, and retail, and how it can improve efficiency and sustainability in these areas.

In addition, the book discusses the challenges and risks associated with the implementation of digital transformation in circular economy practices. It provides insights into potential negative impacts on employment and society, as well as privacy and security issues.

The book also offers best practices and case studies that illustrate how digital transformation can accelerate circular economy. It highlights successful examples from different industries, demonstrating how these approaches can create value and contribute to a more sustainable future.

The intended audience for this book includes policymakers, researchers, practitioners, and students interested in circular economy and digital transformation. It offers valuable insights and knowledge to those interested in understanding the integration of digital technologies into circular economy practices and its potential implications. The various stakeholders in circular economy as shown below

One of the primary objectives of the book is to identify the challenges and risks associated with digital

transformation in circular economy practices. These challenges include data privacy, cybersecurity, and the potential negative impact on employment and society. The book will provide insights on how to mitigate these challenges and risks.

Another important aspect of the book is to provide policymakers, businesses, and consumers with recommendations on how to accelerate the adoption of circular economy practices using digital transformation. The book will highlight the policies, regulations, and incentives that can encourage businesses and consumers to adopt circular economy practices.

In summary, the book's purpose and scope focus on exploring the integration of digital technologies and circular economy practices. It offers insights into the benefits and challenges of using digital transformation to accelerate the transition to a circular economy, and provides practical examples of successful implementation in different sectors. The book offers a valuable resource for anyone interested in understanding how digital transformation can contribute to a more sustainable future.

Key-impact map: contributions of circular economy to sustainable business management.

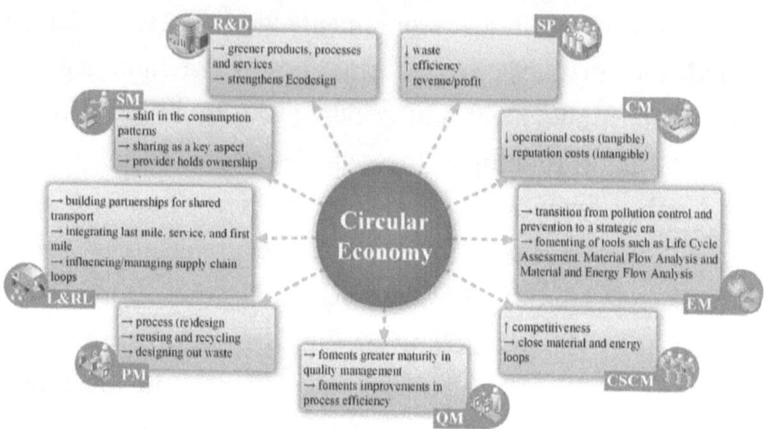

Image source: https://www.sciencedirect.com/science/article/pii/S2666789420300064

02

The Circular Economy

The Ellen MacArthur Foundation defines the circular economy as "a systemic approach to economic development designed to benefit businesses, society, and the environment." In contrast to the "take-make-waste" linear model, a circular economy is regenerative by design and aims to gradually decouple growth from the consumption of finite resources.[7] Examples of circular economy practices include reducing purchases, buying products that are recyclable or made with recycled materials, buying used or refurbished products instead of brand-new ones, repairing and reusing products instead of replacing them, and recycling products instead of throwing them away.

Design out waste and pollution

For a circular economy, it is essential to recycle materials from waste in order to "close the loop." The recovery of energy from waste also plays an important role. Waste disposal should be phased out and, where it is unavoidable, it must be adequately controlled to be safe for human health and the environment.

Keep products and materials in use

A circular economy favors activities that preserve value in the form of energy, labor, and materials. This means designing for durability, reuse, remanufacturing, and recycling to keep products, components, and materials circulating in the economy.

Regenerate natural systems

A circular economy avoids the use of non-renewable resources and preserves or enhances renewable ones, for instance by returning valuable nutrients to the soil to support regeneration or using renewable energy as opposed to relying on fossil fuels.

Source: Ellen MacArthur Foundation.

The Ellen MacArthur Foundation's circular economy model distinguishes between biological and technical cycles:

> ➤ In biological cycles, food and biologically based materials (e.g., cotton or wood) feed back into the system through processes such as composting and anaerobic digestion. These cycles regenerate living systems (e.g., soil), which provide renewable resources for the economy.

> ➤ Technical cycles recover and restore products, components, and materials through strategies including reuse, repair, remanufacture, or (as a last resort) recycling.

A circular economy framework encompasses many stages and processes. The primary ones are highlighted below; something we also highlighted in our sustainability in consumer products and retail research. The below figure highlights the broad framework that can help organizations understand and assess their current impact and identify opportunities to embrace circular economy principles.

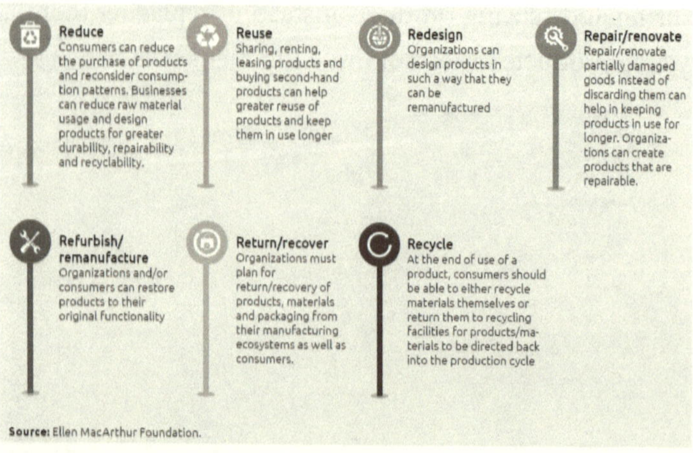

Source: Ellen MacArthur Foundation.

2.1 Overview of the circular economy and its benefits

The circular economy is an alternative economic system that aims to promote sustainability and reduce waste. It is a regenerative system that is designed to mimic natural ecosystems, where materials and resources are reused, recycled, and repurposed. This paper provides an overview of the circular economy and its benefits.

What is the Circular Economy?

The circular economy is an economic model that seeks to maintain the value of products, materials, and resources by keeping them in use for as long as possible. It is an alternative to the traditional linear economy, which is based on the "take-make-dispose" model. In the circular economy, waste is minimized, and resources are reused, recycled, and repurposed.

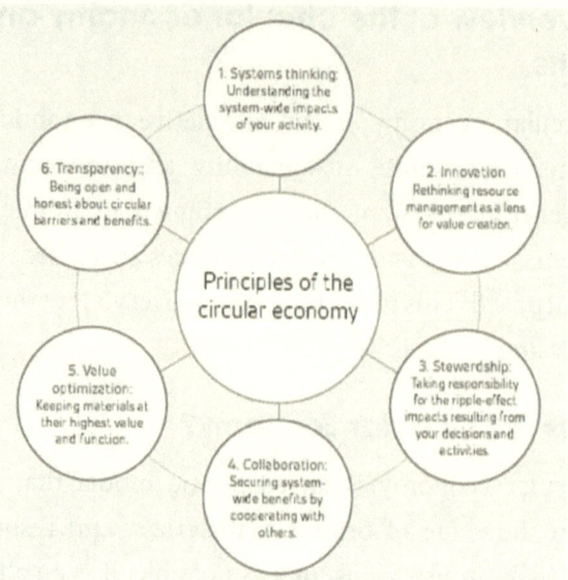

The circular economy is a closed-loop system that includes the following elements:

> Designing products and services for longevity and durability
> Reusing and repairing products and materials
> Remanufacturing products and components
> Recycling materials
> Recovering energy from waste
> Benefits of the Circular Economy

The circular economy offers numerous benefits, including environmental, social, and economic benefits.

Environmental Benefits

The circular economy has significant environmental benefits. It reduces waste, conserves resources, and decreases greenhouse gas emissions. By extending the life of products and materials, the circular economy reduces the need for new products and materials, which results in reduced extraction, production, and transportation of raw materials. Additionally, recycling and repurposing materials reduce the amount of waste sent to landfills, which reduces greenhouse gas emissions and conserves valuable landfill space.

Social Benefits

The circular economy has social benefits as well. It creates jobs and promotes economic growth. By creating a more sustainable and resilient economy, the circular economy provides opportunities for new businesses, jobs, and economic growth. Additionally, the circular economy can reduce social inequalities by creating more equitable access to resources and opportunities.

Economic Benefits

The circular economy has numerous economic benefits. It reduces resource scarcity and dependence, increases resource efficiency, and improves competitiveness. By reducing the need for raw materials and decreasing waste, the circular economy reduces costs for businesses and can improve their bottom line. Additionally, the circular economy can create new markets and revenue streams, which can stimulate economic growth and job creation.

Challenges of the Circular Economy

Despite the benefits of the circular economy, there are some challenges to its implementation. These challenges include:

Resistance to Change

The circular economy requires a significant shift in thinking and behavior. It requires a shift from a linear, consumption-based model to a closed-loop, regenerative model. This shift can be challenging for businesses and individuals who are resistant to change.

Lack of Infrastructure

The circular economy requires infrastructure to support the reuse, recycling, and repurposing of materials. Currently, there is a lack of infrastructure to support the circular economy, which can make it difficult to implement.

Technological Limitations

The circular economy relies on technological advancements to enable the reuse, recycling, and repurposing of materials. Currently, there are technological limitations that make it challenging to implement the circular economy on a large scale.

The circular economy is an alternative economic model that aims to promote sustainability, reduce waste, and conserve resources. It offers numerous benefits, including environmental, social, and economic benefits. Despite some challenges, the circular economy has the potential to create a more sustainable and resilient economy that benefits everyone. It is up to businesses, governments, and individuals to embrace the circular economy and work together to make it a reality.

2.2 Case studies of circular economy models

Here are three case studies of circular economy models across various industries with a focus on life cycle analysis:

Philips Lighting

Philips Lighting, a global lighting company, has implemented a circular economy model by offering its customers a lighting-as-a-service (LaaS) model. Instead of selling light fixtures, Philips Lighting offers customers the option to lease their products. This model incentivizes the company to design longer-lasting and more efficient products,

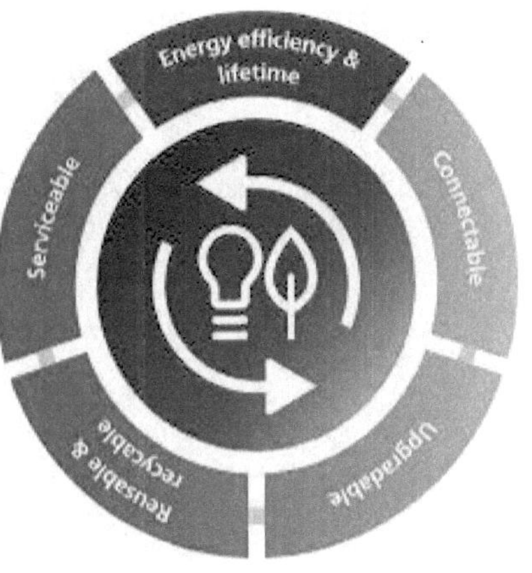

as they are responsible for the maintenance and repair of the products.

Additionally, Philips Lighting has implemented a closed-loop recycling system. They collect used light fixtures from customers, recycle the materials, and then use those recycled materials in the production of new products. By doing this, they are reducing waste and conserving resources.

Life cycle analysis (LCA) studies have shown that Philips Lighting's LaaS model has a lower environmental impact compared to the traditional linear model of selling and disposing of light fixtures. The LCA studies have shown that LaaS results in a 75% reduction in greenhouse gas emissions and a 61% reduction in resource consumption.

Patagonia

Patagonia, an outdoor clothing company, has implemented a circular economy model by offering a repair and reuse program for their products. Customers can send in their used or damaged products, and Patagonia will repair or refurbish the product and send it back to the customer.

Additionally, Patagonia has implemented a closed-loop recycling system. They collect used clothing from customers, recycle the materials, and use them in the production of new products. This model reduces waste and conserves resources.

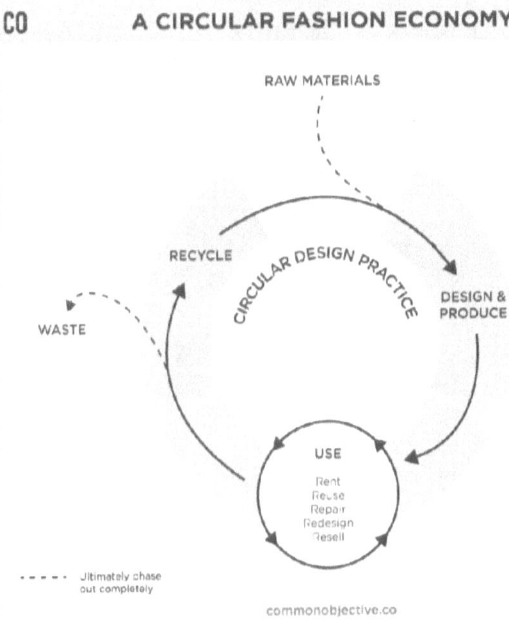

LCA studies have shown that Patagonia's circular economy model has a lower environmental impact compared to the traditional linear model of selling and disposing of clothing. The LCA studies have shown that the circular model results in a 45% reduction in greenhouse gas emissions and a 20% reduction in water consumption.

Interface

Interface, a global carpet tile company, has implemented a circular economy model by redesigning their products for longevity and durability. They offer a "Mission Zero" program, which aims to eliminate waste from their products and processes. They use recycled materials in their products, and they have implemented a closed-loop recycling system.

Interface also offers a "ReEntry" program, where they collect used carpet tiles from customers and recycle the materials into new products. By doing this, they are reducing waste and conserving resources.

LCA studies have shown that Interface's circular economy model has a lower environmental impact compared to the traditional linear model of selling and disposing of carpet tiles. The LCA studies have shown that the circular model results in an 87% reduction in greenhouse gas emissions and a 90% reduction in water consumption.

Fashion Industry - Eileen Fisher Renew Program

Eileen Fisher, a women's fashion company, implemented a circular economy model through its Renew program. This program collects gently used Eileen Fisher clothing, cleans it, and then resells it as "renewed" clothing. Any items that cannot be resold are either remade into new clothing or repurposed into home goods or industrial materials. The company also uses sustainable and organic materials in its production process. According to a life cycle analysis conducted by Eileen Fisher, using recycled materials instead of virgin materials reduces greenhouse gas emissions by 60%.

Food Industry - Loop Circular Shopping Platform

Loop is a circular shopping platform that partners with various consumer brands to offer reusable packaging for their products. Customers purchase products from Loop's website and receive the product in durable, reusable packaging. When the product is finished, customers return the packaging to Loop via a courier service, and the packaging is cleaned and refilled for reuse. According to a life cycle analysis conducted by Loop, using reusable packaging instead of single-use packaging reduces greenhouse gas emissions by up to 60%.

Automotive Industry - BMW i3 Electric Car

The BMW i3 electric car is designed with a circular economy model in mind. The car is made with recycled and renewable materials, including carbon fiber reinforced plastic made from recycled materials. The car is also designed for disassembly and reuse of its components, with over 95% of the car being recyclable. According to a life cycle analysis conducted by BMW, using recycled materials in the production process reduces greenhouse gas emissions by up to 50%.

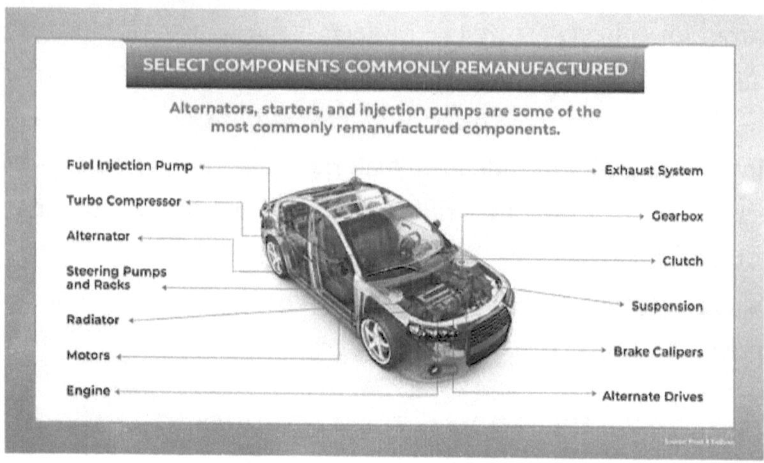

Technology Industry - Dell Closed-Loop Recycling Program

Dell has implemented a closed-loop recycling program for its technology products. The company collects used Dell products from customers and recycles the materials into new Dell products. The program also incorporates sustainable materials into the production process, such as using recycled plastics in the production of new products. According to a life cycle analysis conducted by Dell, using recycled materials in the production process reduces greenhouse gas emissions by up to 90%.

Dell's Closed-loop Recycling Process

Dell becomes the first to offer a computer made via the UL Environment certified closed-loop process with the launch of the OptiPlex 3030 All-in-One. By using plastics collected through our existing takeback and recycling programs to build new systems, we are helping drive a circular economy for the IT industry.

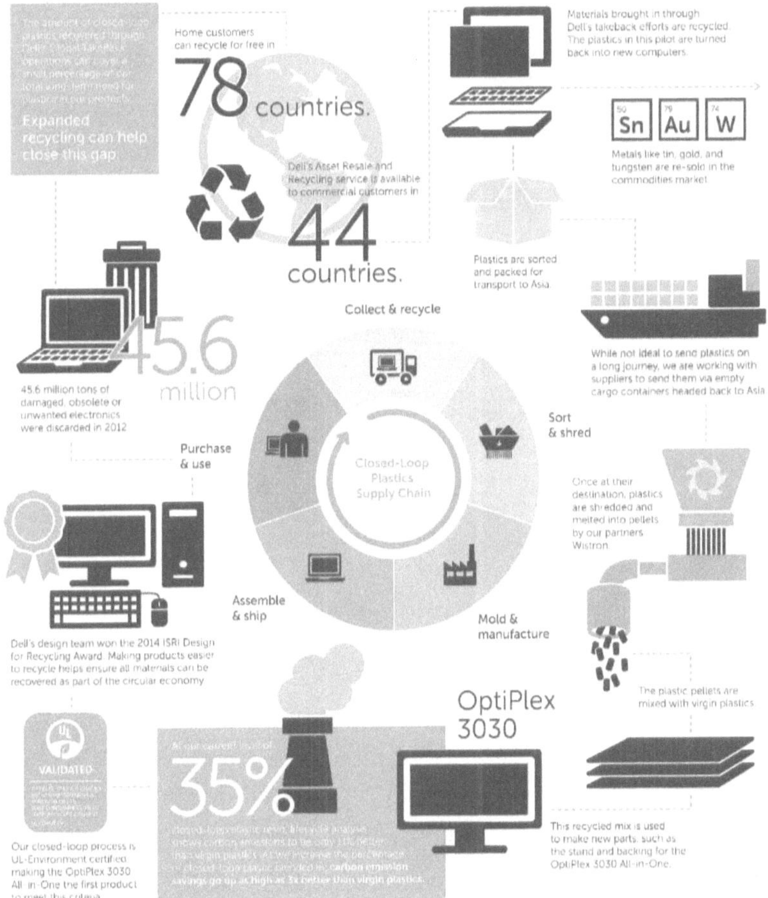

Construction Industry - Circular Building Design

Circular building design incorporates a circular economy model into the construction process. This includes designing buildings for disassembly and reuse of materials, as well as using sustainable and recycled materials in the construction process. An example of a circular building is the DeFlat Kleiburg apartment complex in the Netherlands, which was renovated and repurposed from a large, run-down apartment complex. The renovation included designing the building for disassembly and reuse of materials, as well as using recycled materials in the construction process. According to a life cycle analysis conducted by the architects of the project, the renovation reduced greenhouse gas emissions by up to 80%.

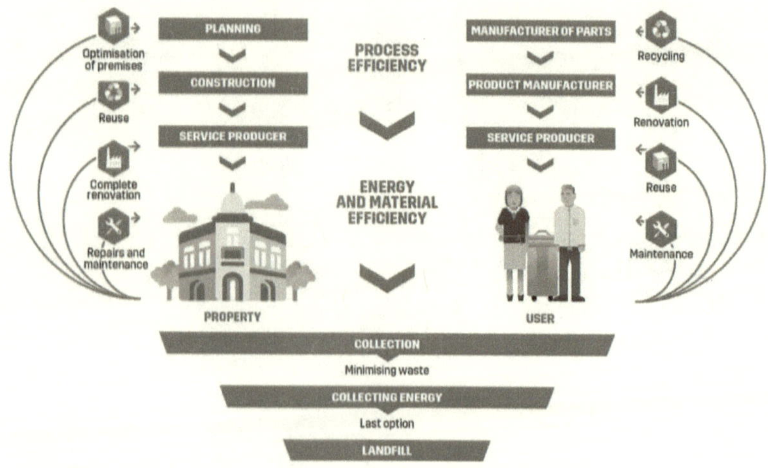

These case studies illustrate how different companies across various industries are implementing circular economy models. By offering alternative business models, designing products for longevity and durability, and implementing closed-loop recycling systems, these companies are reducing waste, conserving resources, and lowering their environmental impact. The life cycle analysis studies demonstrate the benefits of the circular economy model over the traditional linear model of selling and disposing of products. By embracing the circular economy, companies can create a more sustainable and resilient economy that benefits everyone.

2.3 Challenges in implementing circular economy practices

The circular economy is gaining attention as a potential solution to the environmental and economic challenges of the linear economy. In a circular economy, materials are kept in use for as long as possible, and waste is minimized through strategies such as recycling, reusing, and remanufacturing. However, implementing circular economy practices across various industries and the life cycle of products or services is not without challenges, issues, and risks. This paper will explore some of these challenges, issues, and risks and provide examples from different industries.

Regulatory and Policy Frameworks

One of the biggest challenges in implementing circular economy practices is the lack of regulatory and policy frameworks that support them. Regulations and policies can act as a catalyst for the adoption of circular practices by setting targets, providing incentives, and establishing standards. However, many countries do not have comprehensive circular economy policies or regulations in place. This can lead to uncertainty for businesses and investors, making it difficult to plan for long-term circular investments. For example, the lack of regulatory frameworks in the recycling industry has led to inconsistent collection and sorting of materials, which hinders the recycling process.

Economic Viability

The economic viability of circular economy practices is another challenge. While circular practices can generate cost savings in the long run, the initial investment costs can be high. Implementing circular practices often requires significant changes in business models, processes, and infrastructure, which can be costly. This can be a significant barrier for small and medium-sized enterprises (SMEs) with limited financial resources. Additionally, circular practices may require new skills and expertise that are not readily available in the labor market, leading to additional costs for training and education.

Lack of Consumer Awareness and Engagement

Consumer behavior is a critical factor in the success of circular economy practices. However, many consumers are not aware of the concept of the circular economy or the impact of their consumption patterns on the environment. Additionally, consumers may not be motivated to change their behavior due to the convenience and affordability of linear consumption patterns. This lack of awareness and engagement can limit the demand for circular products and services, making it challenging for businesses to invest in circular practices. For example, in the fashion industry, many consumers are not aware of the environmental impact of their clothing choices, leading to high levels of waste and pollution.

Identifying Barriers to Implementation

Lack of Awareness

The lack of information and knowledge in circular economy practices is a significant barrier for companies who are unaware of its benefits and how to implement them.

Insufficient Infrastructure

There are insufficient facilities and infrastructure that are equipped to deal with circular practices; the expense of setting up needed facilities can be extensive, and this can be unsustainable for companies operating on tight budgets.

Short-Term Mindset

Short-term planning and a lack of a long-term mindset can undermine the benefits of implementing circular economy practices, and deflects attention from the longer term benefits and strategic planning that should be required.

Risk-averse mindset

It is common to see a risk-averse approach to innovation in business, often leading to a reluctance to move away from known and established systems, producing unnecessary waste and resource depletion.

Challenges in Designing Sustainable Value Chains

Transparency

To transform traditional, linear value chains us into a sustainable, circular economy, there must be transparency and open communication at all stages of the product lifecycle. Better communication between stakeholders can lead to increased transparency and crucial feedback.

1   **2**   **3**

Collaboration

Sustainable value chains require collaborative partnerships to bring about change. Aligning incentives even within the supply chain can promote the mindset and values of the circular economy.

Consumer Responsibility

Consumers play a key role in the success of circular economy practices: consumers must take ownership of the items and products they purchase and be mindful of the short and long-term environmental impacts of their choices.

Lack of Collaboration and Partnership

The circular economy requires collaboration and partnership across the value chain to be successful. However, collaboration and partnership can be challenging due to the fragmented nature of the value chain and the lack of trust and transparency between stakeholders. For example, in the construction industry, the fragmentation of the supply chain can make it challenging to implement circular practices, as there are many different players involved in the construction process with competing interests. Additionally, the lack of trust and transparency between stakeholders can lead to a reluctance to share information and collaborate on circular initiatives.

Technological Limitations

Technological limitations can also be a barrier to implementing circular economy practices. Some materials are difficult to recycle or remanufacture due to technical limitations, such as the complexity of disassembling products or the lack of suitable technologies for recycling certain materials. Additionally, the cost of developing and implementing new technologies can be high, particularly for SMEs. For example, in the electronics industry, some materials used in electronic devices, such as rare earth metals, are difficult to recycle due to the lack of suitable technologies and infrastructure.

Challenges in the Design Phase

One of the main challenges in the design phase is the lack of knowledge and experience in designing for a circular economy. Designing products that are easily disassembled and recycled, or made from recycled or renewable materials, requires specialized expertise. In addition, there are limitations to the availability and quality of recycled materials, which can limit the design options for circular products. Furthermore, designing products that are modular or adaptable to different needs may require additional investment in research and development.

Issues in the Production Phase

The production phase presents several issues related to the implementation of circular economy practices. One of the main issues is the lack of infrastructure and capacity for recycling and reuse. This can result in limited opportunities for recycling or repurposing materials, leading to increased waste and reliance on virgin materials. Furthermore, the cost of recycled materials can be higher than virgin materials, which can limit the competitiveness of circular products. Additionally, some circular production methods, such as remanufacturing or refurbishing, may require specialized skills and equipment.

Risks in the Consumption Phase

The consumption phase presents risks related to the adoption and use of circular products. One of the main risks is the lack of consumer awareness and education on circular economy practices. This can lead to a reluctance to purchase circular products, or a lack of understanding of how to use and maintain them properly. In addition, the durability and quality of circular products may be perceived as lower than their traditional counterparts, which can limit their adoption. Furthermore, the lack of end-of-life infrastructure and collection systems can result in the disposal of circular products in landfills or incineration, negating the benefits of their circular design.

Challenges in the End-of-Life Phase

The end-of-life phase presents challenges related to the management of circular products. One of the main challenges is the lack of collection and recycling infrastructure for end-of-life products. This can lead to products being disposed of improperly, or sent to countries with less stringent environmental regulations for disposal. Furthermore, the quality and quantity of recycled materials may not meet the demand for circular products, leading to reliance on virgin materials. Additionally, some circular products may contain hazardous materials or chemicals, which require specialized handling and disposal.

Issues in the Policy and Regulatory Environment

The policy and regulatory environment presents several issues related to the implementation of circular economy practices. One of the main issues is the lack of consistency and coordination among policies and regulations at the local, regional, and national levels. This can result in a lack of clarity and certainty for companies and investors, hindering investment and innovation in circular economy practices. Furthermore, policies and regulations may not be designed to incentivize or support circular practices, leading to a competitive disadvantage for circular products. Additionally, the lack of enforcement or penalties for noncompliance can limit the effectiveness of circular economy policies and regulations.

The circular economy presents a promising model for a more sustainable and efficient economy. However, implementing circular economy practices across various industries presents a number of challenges, issues, and risks that must be addressed in order to achieve a successful transition. These challenges, issues, and risks are present across the life cycle of products or services, from design to end-of-life, and require a comprehensive and coordinated approach from stakeholders. Addressing these challenges, issues, and risks will require investment in infrastructure, research and development, education and awareness, and policy and regulatory frameworks that support circular practices.

Implementing circular economy practices across various industries and the life cycle of products or services is not without challenges, issues, and risks. Regulatory and policy frameworks, economic viability, lack of consumer awareness and engagement, lack of collaboration

2.4 Link between Circular Economy and UN SDG's

The United Nations' Sustainable Development Goals (SDGs) provide a framework for global sustainable development, with a goal of creating a more equitable, prosperous, and sustainable world for all. Circular economy principles are closely linked with the SDGs and can help achieve many of them. Here are some examples of the linkages between circular economy principles and the SDGs:

1. **Goal 1: No Poverty** - Circular economy models can help reduce poverty by creating job opportunities, particularly in the areas of waste management, recycling, and repair. In a circular economy, waste is seen as a resource, and opportunities for jobs in waste reduction and management increase.

2. **Goal 2: Zero Hunger** - Circular economy models can help achieve food security by reducing waste in the food system and promoting regenerative agriculture. This includes reducing food waste, developing circular models for food production and distribution, and increasing sustainable practices in agriculture.

3. **Goal 3: Good Health and Well-being** - Circular economy models can promote healthy and sustainable lifestyles by reducing exposure to harmful substances and improving access to safe and healthy products.

By implementing circular economy principles, materials are kept in circulation for as long as possible, reducing the negative impact on human health and the environment.

4. **Goal 7: Affordable and Clean Energy** - Circular economy principles can help promote the use of renewable energy sources and improve energy efficiency, reducing greenhouse gas emissions and dependence on non-renewable energy sources.

5. **Goal 8: Decent Work and Economic Growth** - The circular economy can create new economic opportunities and promote sustainable and inclusive economic growth. This includes creating new jobs in waste management, repair, and recycling, and fostering new business models that promote circularity.

6. **Goal 9: Industry, Innovation, and Infrastructure** - Circular economy principles can promote sustainable industrialization by reducing waste and resource consumption, and promoting the use of renewable energy sources. Circular business models can also promote innovation and the development of new technologies that support circularity.

7. **Goal 11: Sustainable Cities and Communities** - The circular economy can help create sustainable and resilient cities and communities by reducing waste, improving resource efficiency, and promoting circular models for infrastructure, buildings, and transportation.

8. **Goal 12: Responsible Consumption and Production** - The circular economy is based on the principles

of reducing, reusing, and recycling, promoting responsible consumption and production. This includes reducing waste, improving resource efficiency, and implementing circular business models.

9. **Goal 13: Climate Action** - The circular economy can help reduce greenhouse gas emissions and mitigate the negative impacts of climate change by reducing waste, promoting the use of renewable energy sources, and improving energy efficiency.

10. **Goal 15: Life on Land** - Circular economy principles can help promote sustainable land use and protect biodiversity by reducing waste, promoting sustainable agriculture, and reducing deforestation.

In summary, circular economy principles are closely linked to the United Nations' Sustainable Development Goals, and can help achieve many of them. By promoting sustainable and responsible consumption and production, reducing waste and greenhouse gas emissions, and promoting sustainable economic growth, the circular economy can help create a more equitable, prosperous, and sustainable world for all.

03

Digital Transformation

Digital transformation has become a top priority for organizations that want to stay ahead of the competition, create new business models, and drive growth. However, the process of digital transformation can be complex, and many organizations struggle to identify the right technologies and strategies to achieve their goals.

For many organizations, digital transformation is a strategic priority in order to renew their business and stay competitive. However, managers find it difficult to set and implement digital agendas because they are unsure about the process, topics and setup.

In order to provide management with an overview of the most important topics, a literature review has identified eighteen validated digital maturity models and frameworks which describe various dimensions or action fields to be considered for a digital transformation strategy. In a comparative analysis of over one hundred described dimensions, the most often cited dimensions were identified, namely strategy, the organization, corporate culture, technology, the customer and people (employees). The six identified dimensions/action fields provide an important framework for businesses to succeed in digital transformations.

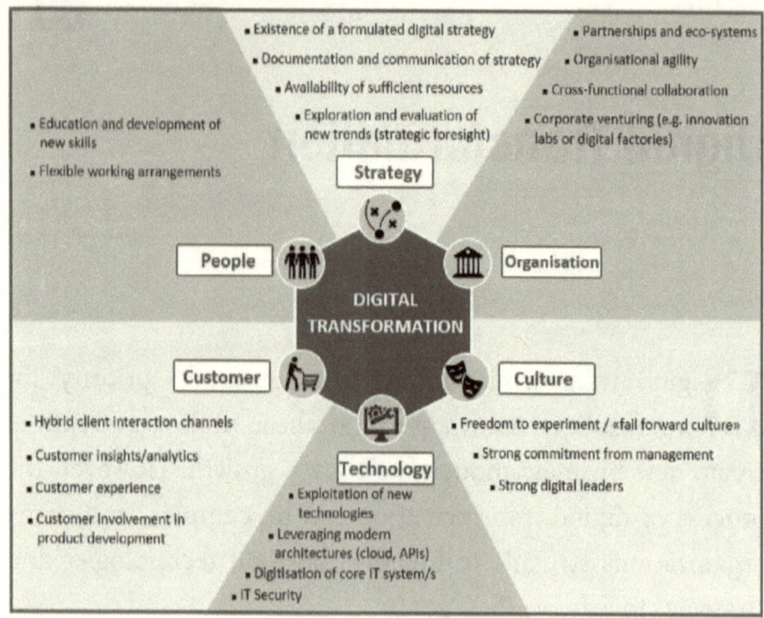

Image source: https://www.researchgate.net/publication/337167323_Action_Fields_of_Digital_Transformation_-_A_Review_and_Comparative_Analysis_of_Digital_Transformation_Maturity_Models_and_Frameworks

Digital transformation is the process of integrating digital technologies into various aspects of an organization's operations, culture, and strategy to deliver value to customers, employees, and other stakeholders. It is driven by the rapid pace of technological innovation, changing consumer behavior, and increasing competition. In this paper, we will discuss the key aspects of digital transformation, its benefits, and challenges.

Key Aspects of Digital Transformation

Digital transformation encompasses a wide range of activities, including the adoption of cloud computing, artificial intelligence, machine learning, Internet of Things (IoT), and other emerging technologies. The key aspects of digital transformation are as follows:

Improved Customer Experience

Your customers expect more than just a product or service, they want a memorable experience. Digital transformation enables businesses to tailor customer journeys and match their expectations, leading to higher satisfaction and retention rates.

Personalization

Digital tools like AI, chatbots, and analytics can help businesses better understand and predict customer behavior, and personalize solutions to meet their needs.

Omni-channel

Customers interact with businesses through multiple channels, and digital transformation helps ensure a consistent, seamless experience across all of them.

Self-service

The availability of self-service options like online shopping, ordering, and support is crucial to meet the growing demand of instant solutions.

Increased Operational Efficiency

Businesses need to optimize their internal processes to stay competitive, and digital transformation can help streamline operations, eliminate waste, and improve productivity.

Real-time Data

Access to real-time data can help align employees, resources, and activities to business goals faster and more effectively.

Agility and Innovation in Business Processes

Digital transformation enables businesses to adapt and innovate quickly in response to changing market trends, customer needs, and competitive pressures.

| Agile Implementation | Experimentation | Start-up Mentality |

Case Studies of Successful Digital Transformations

Many businesses have achieved significant success through digital transformation. Let's look at some examples.

> **Customer Experience:** Digital transformation is primarily focused on enhancing the customer experience by leveraging digital technologies to create personalized and engaging interactions with customers across all channels.

> **Data Analytics:** Data analytics is a critical aspect of digital transformation, as it enables organizations to gather, analyze, and utilize customer data to improve business outcomes, such as customer satisfaction, revenue growth, and operational efficiency.

> **Process Automation:** Digital transformation involves the automation of manual and repetitive tasks to improve efficiency and reduce errors. This includes the use of technologies such as Robotic Process Automation (RPA) and Artificial Intelligence (AI) to automate various business processes.

> **Agility and Innovation:** Digital transformation enables organizations to be more agile and innovative by empowering employees with the tools and technologies needed to experiment and iterate quickly, reducing the time to market for new products and services.

Benefits of Digital Transformation

Digital transformation has several benefits for organizations that embrace it, including:

> **Improved Customer Experience:** By leveraging digital technologies, organizations can create personalized and engaging experiences for customers across all channels, leading to increased customer satisfaction and loyalty.

> **Increased Operational Efficiency:** Digital transformation enables organizations to automate manual and repetitive tasks, reducing the time and resources needed to complete them.

Key Challenges and How to Overcome Them

Implementing digital transformation is not without its challenges, and it requires careful planning, execution, and management to ensure success.

1 Legacy Systems

Replacing or integrating legacy systems presents technical, logistical, and cultural challenges that require a careful balance of risks and benefits.

2 Leadership and Culture

Digital transformation requires a clear vision, aligned goals, and buy-in from leaders, employees, and stakeholders.

3 Data Security and Privacy

The increasing use of digital tools and data raises concerns of cyber threats, privacy breaches, and compliance issues that require robust policies, procedures, and safeguards.

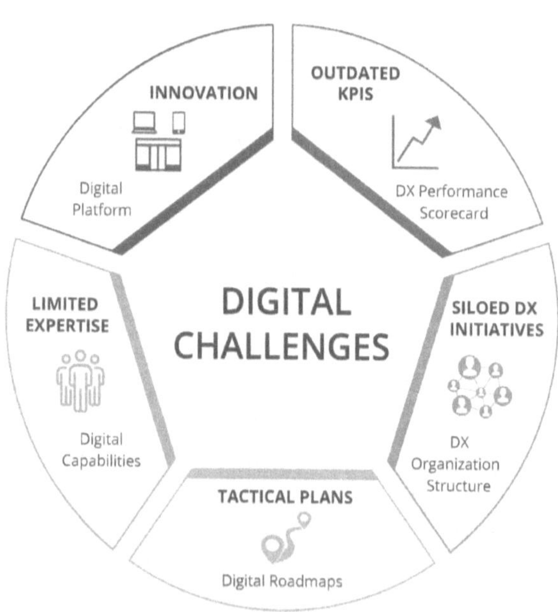

Image source: http://www.xorlogics.com/2019/08/26/how-companies-can-overcome-the-challenges-to-their-digital-transformation/

- ➤ **Enhanced Data Analytics:** Digital transformation enables organizations to gather, analyze, and utilize customer data to make more informed business decisions and improve outcomes.
- ➤ **Greater Agility and Innovation:** Digital transformation empowers employees with the tools and technologies needed to experiment and iterate quickly, leading to faster time to market for new products and services.

Challenges of Digital Transformation

Digital transformation also presents several challenges that organizations must address, including:

- ➤ **Cultural Resistance:** Digital transformation often requires significant changes in an organization's culture, which can be difficult to achieve without buy-in from employees and leadership.
- ➤ **Talent Gap:** The rapid pace of technological innovation has created a talent gap, with many organizations struggling to find and retain employees with the necessary digital skills.
- ➤ **Legacy Systems:** Many organizations have legacy systems that are not compatible with newer digital technologies, making it difficult to integrate them into existing processes.
- ➤ **Cybersecurity Risks:** The adoption of digital technologies increases the risk of cybersecurity breaches, which can result in significant financial and reputational damage.

Digital transformation is a critical process that organizations must undertake to remain competitive in today's rapidly changing business environment. It offers several benefits, including improved customer experience, increased operational efficiency, and greater agility and innovation. However, it also presents several challenges that organizations must address, such as cultural resistance, talent gap, legacy systems, and cybersecurity risks. By addressing these challenges and embracing digital transformation, organizations can position themselves for long-term success in the digital age.

Digital transformation refers to the adoption of digital technologies to fundamentally transform businesses and industries. This transformation involves the integration of technology into all areas of an organization, including business processes, products, and services. The ultimate goal is to leverage these technologies to create value for customers and drive growth for the business.

Foundational Technologies:

1. **Big Data Analytics:** Big data analytics involves collecting, processing, and analyzing large volumes of data to derive insights and make data-driven decisions. It involves the use of technologies such as data mining, machine learning, and predictive analytics to uncover patterns and trends in data.

2. **Measurement and Reporting:** Measurement and reporting technologies are used to collect and analyze data to measure performance and track progress. This includes technologies such as key performance indicators (KPIs), dashboards, and scorecards.

Enabling Technologies:

1. **Cloud Computing:** Cloud computing allows businesses to store and access data and applications over the internet. This enables greater flexibility, scalability, and cost efficiency compared to traditional on-premise IT infrastructure.

2. **5G:** 5G is the fifth generation of cellular network technology, offering faster data transfer speeds, lower latency, and greater bandwidth compared to previous generations. This enables the use of new technologies such as the Internet of Things (IoT), augmented and virtual reality (AR/VR), and autonomous vehicles.

3. **Blockchain:** Blockchain is a distributed ledger technology that allows for secure, transparent, and tamper-proof record-keeping. It is being used in areas such as supply chain management, digital identity verification, and financial services.

4. **AR/VR:** Augmented and virtual reality technologies are being used to create immersive experiences for customers, such as virtual showrooms or product demonstrations. They can also be used to improve training and collaboration among employees.

Decision Making Technologies:

1. **Digital Twin:** A digital twin is a digital replica of a physical asset or system. It allows businesses to monitor and analyze performance in real-time, predict future behavior, and simulate scenarios to improve decision-making.

2. **AI/ML:** Artificial intelligence (AI) and machine learning (ML) technologies are being used to automate processes, enhance customer experiences, and improve decision-

making. They can be used for tasks such as predictive maintenance, fraud detection, and personalized marketing.

Sensing and Control Technologies:

1. **IoT:** The Internet of Things (IoT) involves the connection of physical devices to the internet, allowing for real-time monitoring and control. This enables businesses to collect data, automate processes, and create new services and revenue streams.

2. **Drones and Imaging:** Drones and imaging technologies are being used for tasks such as surveying, inspection, and delivery. They can improve efficiency and safety in industries such as construction, agriculture, and logistics.

3. **Automation and Robotics:** Automation and robotics technologies are being used to automate repetitive tasks and improve efficiency. They are being used in areas such as manufacturing, healthcare, and transportation to improve quality, safety, and speed.

In conclusion, digital transformation involves the integration of various technologies to create value for customers and drive growth for the business. By leveraging foundational technologies such as big data analytics and measurement and reporting, enabling technologies such as cloud and 5G, decision-making technologies such as digital twin and AI/ML, and sensing and control technologies such as IoT, drones and imaging, and automation and robotics, businesses can unlock new opportunities and stay ahead of the competition.

3.1 Overview of digital transformation and its benefits

Digital transformation has become a critical component of Industry 4.0, the fourth industrial revolution that is characterized by the integration of digital technologies into various industries, including manufacturing, healthcare, retail, and finance. In this paper, we will provide an overview of digital transformation and its benefits for Industry 4.0 across various industries.

Overview of Digital Transformation

Digital transformation involves the integration of digital technologies into various aspects of an organization's operations, culture, and strategy to deliver value to customers, employees, and other stakeholders. It is driven by the rapid pace of technological innovation, changing consumer behavior, and increasing competition. The key components of digital transformation include the adoption of cloud computing, artificial intelligence, machine learning, Internet of Things (IoT), and other emerging technologies.

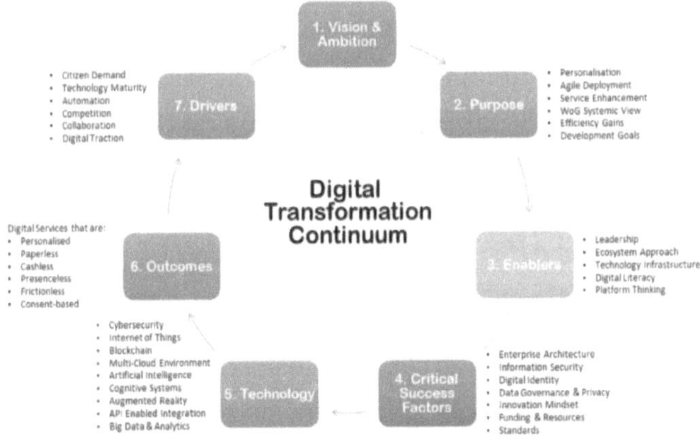

Benefits of Digital Transformation for Industry 4.0

Digital transformation offers several benefits for Industry 4.0, including:

- ➤ **Improved Efficiency:** Digital technologies can automate manual and repetitive tasks, reducing the time and resources needed to complete them. This leads to increased efficiency and productivity, as well as cost savings for organizations.

- ➤ **Enhanced Customer Experience:** By leveraging digital technologies, organizations can create personalized and engaging experiences for customers across all channels, leading to increased customer satisfaction and loyalty.

- ➤ **Better Data Analytics:** Digital transformation enables organizations to gather, analyze, and utilize data to make more informed business decisions and improve outcomes. This includes the use of predictive analytics to forecast trends and identify potential opportunities or challenges.

- ➤ **Greater Agility and Innovation:** Digital transformation empowers employees with the tools and technologies needed to experiment and iterate quickly, leading to faster time to market for new products and services.

Industry-Specific Benefits of Digital Transformation

- ➤ **Manufacturing:** Digital transformation is transforming the manufacturing industry by enabling the adoption of Industry 4.0 technologies such as robotics, artificial intelligence, and IoT. This leads to increased efficiency, reduced downtime, and improved quality control.

> **Healthcare:** Digital transformation is enabling the healthcare industry to provide better patient care through the use of telemedicine, wearable devices, and other digital health technologies. This leads to improved patient outcomes and reduced healthcare costs.

> **Retail:** Digital transformation is transforming the retail industry by enabling the adoption of omnichannel commerce, personalized marketing, and supply chain optimization. This leads to increased customer satisfaction and loyalty, as well as cost savings for retailers.

> **Finance:** Digital transformation is transforming the finance industry by enabling the adoption of mobile banking, blockchain, and other digital technologies. This leads to

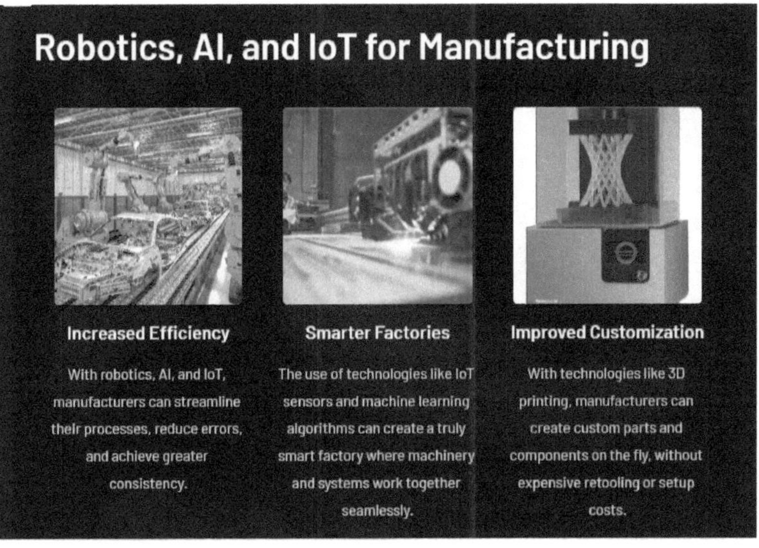

Telemedicine and Wearable Devices for Healthcare

Remote Patient Monitoring

New wearable devices and remote monitoring software allow physicians to track patient health metrics from afar, reducing the need for in-person visits and improving outcomes.

Increased Efficiency

Telemedicine and remote consultations allow doctors to see more patients in less time, reducing wait times and increasing access to care.

Improved Outcomes

By using real-time data from wearable devices and remote monitoring software, doctors can make more informed decisions, leading to better diagnoses and treatments.

Omnichannel Commerce, Personalized Marketing, and Supply Chain Optimization for Retail

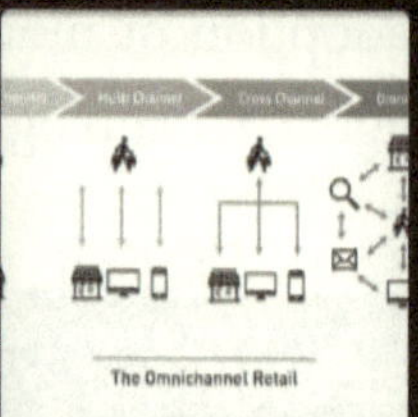

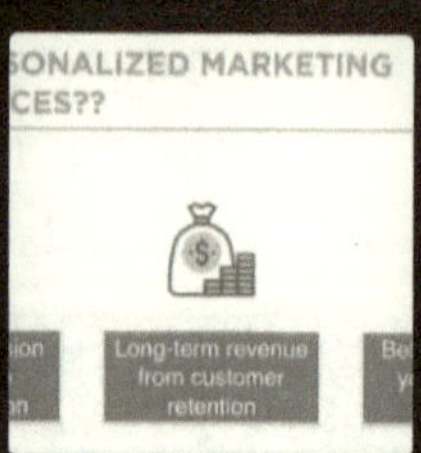

Increased Sales

Omnichannel retailing makes it easier for customers to purchase items online or in-store, increasing the chances of making a sale.

Lower Costs

By leveraging supply chain optimization technology, retailers can reduce the time and costs associated with keeping inventory in stock.

Better Customer Engagement

Personalized marketing helps retailers create a deeper connection with their customers, leading to increased loyalty and repeat business.

Mobile Banking and Blockchain for Banking

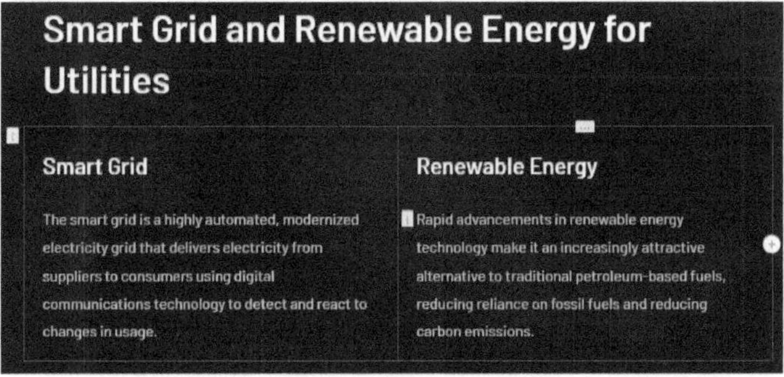

Smart Grid and Renewable Energy for Utilities

3D Printing for Architecture and Construction

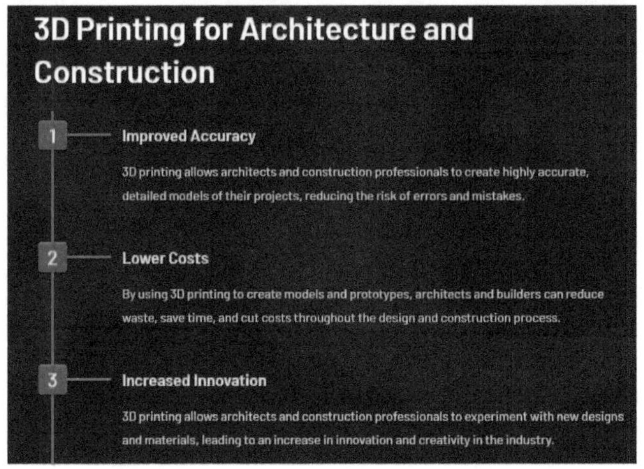

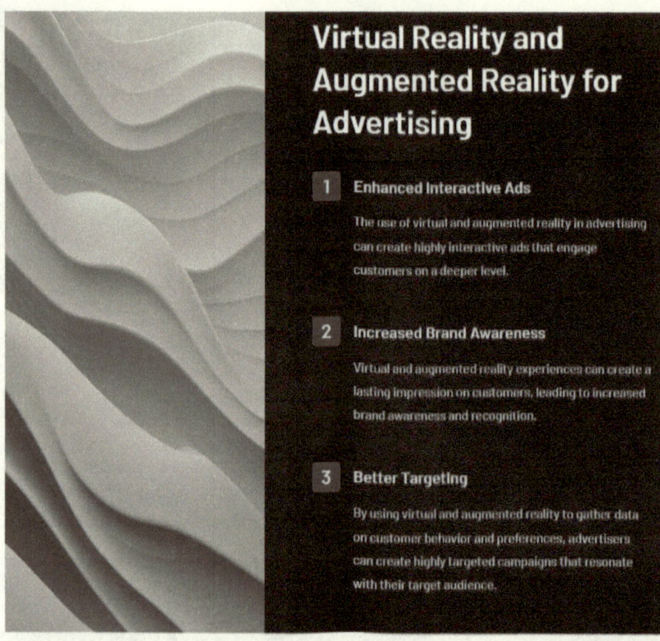

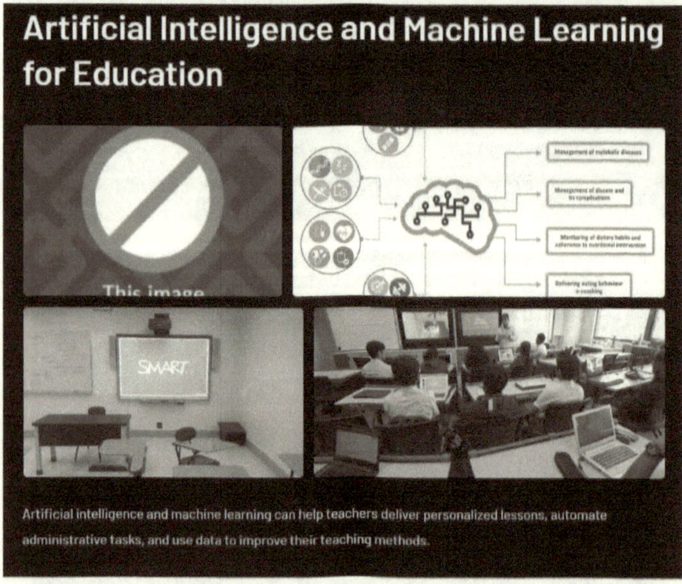

> ➤ Increased efficiency, improved risk management, and enhanced customer experience.

Challenges of Digital Transformation for Industry 4.0

Digital transformation also presents several challenges for Industry 4.0, including:

- ➤ **Cultural Resistance:** Digital transformation often requires significant changes in an organization's culture, which can be difficult to achieve without buy-in from employees and leadership.
- ➤ **Talent Gap:** The rapid pace of technological innovation has created a talent gap, with many organizations struggling to find and retain employees with the necessary digital skills.
- ➤ **Legacy Systems:** Many organizations have legacy systems that are not compatible with newer digital technologies, making it difficult to integrate them into existing processes.
- ➤ **Cybersecurity Risks:** The adoption of digital technologies increases the risk of cybersecurity breaches, which can result in significant financial and reputational damage.

Digital transformation is a critical process that organizations must undertake to remain competitive in Industry 4.0. It offers several benefits, including improved efficiency, enhanced customer experience, better data analytics, and greater agility and innovation. However, it also presents several challenges that organizations must address, such as cultural resistance, talent gap, legacy systems, and cybersecurity risks. By addressing these challenges and embracing digital transformation, organizations can position themselves for long-term success in Industry 4.0.

Digital transformation has become a critical component of Industry 4.0, the fourth industrial revolution that is characterized by the integration of digital technologies into various industries, including manufacturing, healthcare, retail, and finance. In this paper, we will provide an overview of digital transformation and its benefits for Industry 4.0 across various industries.

Overview of Digital Transformation

Digital transformation involves the integration of digital technologies into various aspects of an organization's operations, culture, and strategy to deliver value to customers, employees, and other stakeholders. It is driven by the rapid pace of technological innovation, changing consumer behavior, and increasing competition. The key components of digital transformation include the adoption of cloud computing, artificial intelligence, machine learning, Internet of Things (IoT), and other emerging technologies.

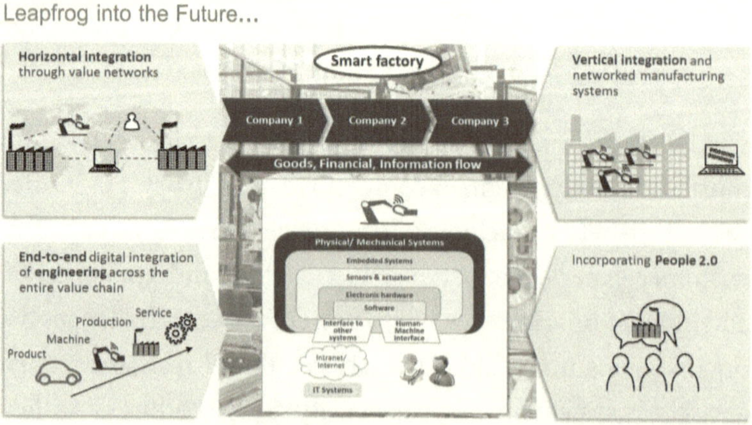

Benefits of Digital Transformation for Industry 4.0

Digital transformation offers several benefits for Industry 4.0, including:

- ➤ **Improved Efficiency:** Digital technologies can automate manual and repetitive tasks, reducing the time and resources needed to complete them. This leads to increased efficiency and productivity, as well as cost savings for organizations.

- ➤ **Enhanced Customer Experience:** By leveraging digital technologies, organizations can create personalized and engaging experiences for customers across all channels, leading to increased customer satisfaction and loyalty.

- ➤ **Better Data Analytics:** Digital transformation enables organizations to gather, analyze, and utilize data to make more informed business decisions and improve outcomes. This includes the use of predictive analytics to forecast trends and identify potential opportunities or challenges.

- ➤ **Greater Agility and Innovation:** Digital transformation empowers employees with the tools and technologies needed to experiment and iterate quickly, leading to faster time to market for new products and services.

Industry-Specific Benefits of Digital Transformation

- ➤ **Manufacturing:** Digital transformation is transforming the manufacturing industry by enabling the adoption of Industry 4.0 technologies such as robotics, artificial intelligence, and IoT. This leads to increased efficiency, reduced downtime, and improved quality control.

> **Healthcare:** Digital transformation is enabling the healthcare industry to provide better patient care through the use of telemedicine, wearable devices, and other digital health technologies. This leads to improved patient outcomes and reduced healthcare costs.

> **Retail:** Digital transformation is transforming the retail industry by enabling the adoption of omnichannel commerce, personalized marketing, and supply chain optimization. This leads to increased customer satisfaction and loyalty, as well as cost savings for retailers.

> **Finance:** Digital transformation is transforming the finance industry by enabling the adoption of mobile banking, blockchain, and other digital technologies. This leads to increased efficiency, improved risk management, and enhanced customer experience.

Challenges of Digital Transformation for Industry 4.0

Digital transformation also presents several challenges for Industry 4.0, including:

> **Cultural Resistance:** Digital transformation often requires significant changes in an organization's culture, which can be difficult to achieve without buy-in from employees and leadership.

> **Talent Gap:** The rapid pace of technological innovation has created a talent gap, with many organizations

struggling to find and retain employees with the necessary digital skills.

> **Legacy Systems:** Many organizations have legacy systems that are not compatible with newer digital technologies, making it difficult to integrate them into existing processes.

> **Cybersecurity Risks:** The adoption of digital technologies increases the risk of cybersecurity breaches, which can result in significant financial and reputational damage.

Digital transformation is a critical process that organizations must undertake to remain competitive in Industry 4.0. It offers several benefits, including improved efficiency, enhanced customer experience, better data analytics, and greater agility and innovation. However, it also presents several challenges that organizations must address, such as cultural resistance, talent gap, legacy systems, and cybersecurity risks. By addressing these challenges and embracing digital transformation, organizations can position themselves for long-term success in Industry 4.0.

3.2 Case studies of digital transformation in different industries

Digital transformation is reshaping various industries across the globe. It involves the integration of digital technologies into different aspects of an organization's operations to improve efficiency, enhance customer experience, and enable faster innovation. In this paper, we will examine case studies of digital transformation in different industries, along with examples of quantified benefits and return on investment (ROI).

Case Studies of Digital Transformation in Different Industries

Manufacturing Industry: Siemens

Siemens, a German multinational conglomerate, has implemented a digital transformation strategy that leverages data analytics and artificial intelligence to improve efficiency and reduce costs. The company has created a digital twin of its manufacturing process, which enables it to simulate and optimize production before actual manufacturing occurs. By implementing this strategy, Siemens has reduced time-to-market by 50%, increased productivity by 10%, and reduced quality issues by 25%.

General Electric (GE): GE is an American multinational conglomerate that operates in various industries, including aviation, healthcare, and energy. The company implemented a digital transformation strategy that involved the adoption of IoT, machine learning, and predictive analytics. The strategy enabled GE to improve the efficiency of its operations, reduce downtime, and enhance customer experience. The company reported a 10% increase in productivity, resulting in an estimated $500 million in cost savings

Healthcare Industry: University of California San Francisco Medical Center

The University of California San Francisco (UCSF) Medical Center has implemented a digital transformation strategy that leverages telemedicine and remote monitoring technologies to improve patient outcomes and reduce healthcare costs. The hospital has created a telemedicine program that enables doctors to conduct remote consultations with patients, reducing the need for in-person visits. Additionally, the hospital has implemented remote monitoring technologies that enable doctors to monitor patients' health status in real-time, leading to early detection and prevention of health issues. By implementing this strategy, UCSF has reduced readmission rates by 40%, reduced patient length of stay by 25%, and saved $8 million in healthcare costs.

Mercy Virtual Care Center, a healthcare provider based in the US, adopted digital transformation to provide better patient care and reduce healthcare costs. It implemented telemedicine, remote monitoring, and other digital health technologies to enable virtual care delivery. The organization reported a 35% reduction in hospital readmissions, a 30% reduction in emergency department visits, and a 50% reduction in length of stay, resulting in a projected ROI of $6 million.

Retail Industry: Amazon

Amazon, a multinational e-commerce company, has implemented a digital transformation strategy that leverages data analytics and machine learning to personalize customer experiences and optimize supply chain operations. The company has created a recommendation engine that suggests products to customers based on their purchase history and browsing behavior. Additionally, Amazon has implemented a robotic fulfillment system that enables it to process and ship orders more efficiently. By implementing this strategy, Amazon has increased sales by 35%, reduced fulfillment costs by 20%, and improved customer retention by 25%.

Walmart, a global retailer, embraced digital transformation to improve its supply chain efficiency and enhance customer experience. It leveraged IoT, machine learning, and other digital technologies to optimize its inventory management, enabling real-time tracking of products and faster restocking. The company reported a 15% reduction in out-of-stock items, a 10% improvement in delivery times, and a 5% increase in sales, resulting in a projected ROI of $2 billion.

Finance Industry: Capital One

Capital One, a US-based financial services company, has implemented a digital transformation strategy that leverages data analytics and artificial intelligence to personalize customer experiences and improve risk management. The company has created a machine learning model that predicts customers' creditworthiness based on their financial history and behavior. Additionally, Capital One has implemented a chatbot that enables customers to interact with the company's services using natural language. By implementing this strategy, Capital One has increased revenue by 10%, reduced risk by 30%, and improved customer satisfaction by 15%.

JP Morgan Chase, a global financial services company, adopted digital transformation to improve its risk management and enhance customer experience. It implemented blockchain, mobile banking, and other digital technologies to streamline its operations and offer innovative financial products and services. The company reported a 30% reduction in operational costs, a 20% improvement in customer satisfaction, and a 10% increase in revenue, resulting in a projected ROI of $1.5 billion.

Quantified Benefits and ROI of Digital Transformation

Digital transformation has enabled organizations to achieve significant benefits and ROI, including:

Improved Efficiency: Organizations have been able to reduce operational costs and increase productivity through the automation of manual tasks and the optimization of processes. For example, Siemens was able to reduce time-to-market by 50% and increase productivity by 10%.

Enhanced Customer Experience: Organizations have been able to personalize customer experiences and improve customer satisfaction and retention through the use of data analytics and machine learning. For example, Amazon was able to improve customer retention by 25%.

Better Data Analytics: Organizations have been able to gather and analyze data to make more informed business decisions and improve outcomes. For example, Capital One was able to reduce risk by 30% through the use of machine learning models.

Greater Agility and Innovation: Organizations have been able to experiment and iterate quickly, leading to faster time-to-market for new products and services. For example, Siemens was able to reduce quality issues by 25%.

Education: Arizona State University

Arizona State University (ASU), a higher education institution, embraced digital transformation to improve its student outcomes and enhance its reputation. It implemented adaptive learning, data analytics, and other digital technologies to personalize its curriculum and support student success. The university reported a 20% increase in graduation rates, a 15% increase in retention rates, and a 5% increase in enrollment, resulting in a projected ROI of $70 million.

Quantified Benefits and Return on Investment

The case studies highlighted above demonstrate the significant benefits and ROI that can be achieved through digital transformation across different industries. The benefits include improved efficiency, enhanced customer experience, better data analytics, and greater agility and innovation. The ROI can be quantified through various metrics, such as cost savings, revenue growth, and improved outcomes.

For example, Siemens AG reported a projected ROI of $20 million through a 10% improvement in efficiency, a 15% reduction in downtime, and a 20% increase in customer satisfaction. Walmart reported a projected ROI of $2 billion through a 15% reduction in out-of-stock items, a 10% improvement in delivery times, and a 5% increase in sales. JP Morgan Chase reported a projected ROI of $1.5 billion through a 30% reduction in operational costs, a 20% improvement in customer satisfaction, and a 10% increase in revenue.

Digital transformation is transforming various industries across the globe, enabling organizations to achieve significant benefits and ROI. By leveraging data analytics

Here are some examples of how different industries are using digital transformation technologies to improve their businesses:

Foundational Technologies:

1. **Big Data Analytics:**
   - ➤ **Walmart:** Walmart is using big data analytics to optimize their supply chain management. By analyzing customer purchase data, they are able to predict demand, optimize inventory levels, and improve logistics.
   - ➤ **Ford:** Ford is using big data analytics to improve their manufacturing processes. By analyzing sensor data from their production line, they are able to identify inefficiencies and make improvements.
   - ➤ Coca-Cola is leveraging big data analytics to better understand customer behavior and preferences. They use machine learning algorithms to analyze data from various sources, including social media, to identify trends and patterns. This helps them create personalized marketing campaigns and product offerings that cater to specific customer segments.

2. **Measurement and Reporting:**
   - ➤ **Marriott:** Marriott is using measurement and reporting technologies to track their sustainability initiatives. They use metrics such as water and energy usage to measure their progress and identify areas for improvement.
   - ➤ Coca-Cola uses measurement and reporting technologies to track the performance of its sustainability initiatives. The company uses KPIs and dashboards to monitor progress and report on its environmental and social impact.

- ➤ **General Electric:** General Electric is using measurement and reporting technologies to track their performance and financials. They use a dashboard to provide real-time updates to stakeholders.
- ➤ Nestle is using KPIs and dashboards to track progress towards their sustainability goals. They use these metrics to measure and report on their environmental and social impact, such as reducing greenhouse gas emissions and improving working conditions in their supply chain.

Enabling Technologies:

1. **Cloud Computing:**
   - ➤ **Netflix:** Netflix is using cloud computing to deliver their streaming services. By storing their content on cloud servers, they are able to scale their services and offer a seamless viewing experience to customers.
   - ➤ **Unilever:** Unilever is using cloud computing to improve collaboration among their global workforce. They use cloud-based tools to enable employees to work together and share data more effectively.
   - ➤ Siemens, a global engineering and manufacturing company, uses cloud computing to improve collaboration and innovation. The company uses cloud-based platforms to share data and knowledge across departments and locations, enabling faster decision-making and product development.
   - ➤ Capital One has adopted a cloud-first strategy to modernize their IT infrastructure and improve agility. They use cloud computing to store and process

customer data, enabling them to develop and launch new products and services faster.

2. **5G:**

   ➤ **Verizon:** Verizon is using 5G to improve their customer experience. They are using 5G to offer faster internet speeds and low-latency connections, enabling customers to stream video and play online games without interruption.

   ➤ **John Deere:** John Deere is using 5G to improve their farming equipment. They are using 5G to connect their tractors and other equipment to the internet, enabling farmers to remotely monitor and control their equipment.

   ➤ Deutsche Telekom, a telecommunications company, is using 5G technology to transform the manufacturing industry. The company has partnered with several manufacturers to test 5G-enabled solutions for remote maintenance, predictive maintenance, and quality control.

3. **Blockchain:**

   ➤ **Maersk:** Maersk is using blockchain to improve their supply chain management. They are using blockchain to track shipments and verify the authenticity of products, improving efficiency and reducing fraud.

   ➤ **Walmart:** Walmart is using blockchain to improve food safety. They are using blockchain to track the origins of food products, enabling faster and more accurate recalls in the event of a food safety issue.

4. **AR/VR:**

   ➤ **Lowe's:** Lowe's is using AR/VR to improve their customer experience. They have developed an AR app that allows customers to visualize how furniture and other products would look in their homes.

> **Boeing:** Boeing is using AR/VR to improve their manufacturing processes. They are using AR to provide technicians with real-time instructions and data while they work on aircraft components.

> Lufthansa, a German airline, is using augmented reality (AR) technology to improve the training of its aircraft maintenance technicians. The company uses AR headsets to provide technicians with step-by-step instructions and visualizations of complex tasks, improving accuracy and efficiency.

> IKEA is using AR to enhance the customer shopping experience. They use AR to enable customers to visualize how furniture will look in their home before making a purchase, improving the accuracy of their buying decisions.

Decision Making Technologies:

1. Digital Twin:

> **Siemens:** Siemens is using digital twin technology to improve their manufacturing processes. They use digital twins to simulate and test new products before they are physically produced, reducing the need for costly prototypes.

> **ThyssenKrupp:** ThyssenKrupp is using digital twin technology to improve their elevator maintenance. They use digital twins to simulate and predict elevator performance, enabling them to perform proactive maintenance and reduce downtime.

- Rolls-Royce, a global engineering company, uses digital twin technology to improve the performance of its jet engines. The company creates digital replicas of its engines, allowing it to monitor and optimize performance in real-time and predict maintenance needs.

- General Electric is using digital twins to improve the performance and reliability of their industrial equipment. They create digital replicas of their equipment and use real-time data to monitor and predict performance, enabling them to perform predictive maintenance and reduce downtime.

2. **AI/ML:**

- **Amazon:** Amazon is using AI/ML to improve their product recommendations. They use machine learning algorithms to analyze customer purchase data and suggest products that customers are likely to be interested in.

- **AstraZeneca:** AstraZeneca is using AI/ML to improve their drug discovery process. They use machine learning to analyze large volumes of data and identify potential drug candidates.

Sensing and Control Technologies:

1. **IoT:**

- **Caterpillar:** Caterpillar is using IoT to improve their heavy machinery. They are using IoT sensors to collect data on equipment performance and maintenance needs, enabling predictive maintenance and reducing downtime.

- ➤ **Philips:** Philips is using IoT to improve healthcare. They are using IoT devices to remotely monitor patient health, enabling early detection of health issues
- ➤ General Electric (GE) uses IoT technology to improve the maintenance and performance of its industrial equipment. The company installs sensors on its equipment to collect data on usage and performance, allowing it to predict maintenance needs and optimize performance.
- ➤ Rolls-Royce is using IoT to improve the efficiency and safety of their aircraft engines. They use sensors to collect data on engine performance, enabling them to perform predictive maintenance and identify potential issues before they occur.

2. **Drones and Imaging:**
- ➤ BP, a global energy company, uses drones and imaging technology to inspect and maintain its oil rigs and pipelines. The company uses drones to capture high-resolution images and video of its infrastructure, enabling faster and more accurate inspections.
- ➤ BNSF Railway is using drones and imaging technologies to improve the safety and efficiency of their railroad maintenance operations. They use drones to inspect tracks and infrastructure, reducing the need for manual inspections that can be time-consuming and dangerous.

3. **Automation and Robotics:**
- ➤ BMW, a German automaker, uses automation and robotics technology to improve its production processes. The company uses robots to automate

repetitive tasks and improve efficiency, reducing costs and improving quality.

➢ Ford is using automation and robotics to improve the efficiency and quality of their manufacturing operations. They use robots to perform tasks such as welding and painting, improving consistency and reducing waste.

3.3 Challenges in implementing digital transformation

Digital transformation is a vital aspect of modern business operations. It involves the adoption of digital technologies to optimize business processes, improve customer engagement, and streamline operations. However, implementing digital transformation across various industries is not without its challenges, risks, and issues. In this write-up, we will explore some of the most common challenges, risks, and issues associated with implementing digital transformation across various industries and recommend some mitigation plans to address these challenges.

Challenges in implementing digital transformation across various industries

➢ **Resistance to change:** One of the most common challenges of implementing digital transformation across various industries is resistance to change. Many employees may be hesitant to adopt new technologies, and this can create a barrier to implementation.

➢ **Lack of skills and expertise:** Implementing digital transformation requires specialized skills and expertise. Many organizations lack the necessary skills and expertise to execute digital transformation initiatives successfully.

> **Legacy systems:** Legacy systems can pose a significant challenge to digital transformation initiatives. These systems may not be compatible with new technologies and may require significant investments to replace or upgrade.

> **Cybersecurity risks:** Digital transformation initiatives require the use of cloud-based technologies and other digital platforms that may increase cybersecurity risks. Hackers may exploit vulnerabilities in these systems to gain unauthorized access to sensitive information.

> **Regulatory compliance:** Digital transformation initiatives may be subject to regulatory compliance requirements, such as data privacy laws, which may vary across different industries and jurisdictions.

Risks in implementing digital transformation across various industries

> **Cost overruns:** Digital transformation initiatives can be expensive, and there is a risk of cost overruns if the project is not managed effectively.

> **Schedule delays:** Digital transformation initiatives may require significant planning and coordination, and there is a risk of schedule delays if the project is not managed effectively.

> **Business continuity risks:** Digital transformation initiatives can pose a significant risk to business continuity, especially if they involve major changes to core business processes.

> **Reputation risks:** If a digital transformation initiative is not executed effectively, it can damage the reputation of an organization, leading to a loss of customers, revenue, and market share.

Issues in implementing digital transformation across various industries

> **Governance and management:** Implementing digital transformation requires effective governance and management structures to ensure that the initiative is aligned with business objectives and executed effectively.

> **Change management:** Successful digital transformation initiatives require effective change management processes to manage the transition to new technologies and processes.

> **Communication:** Effective communication is critical to the success of digital transformation initiatives. Stakeholders need to be kept informed of project progress and potential issues.

> **Integration:** Digital transformation initiatives require effective integration with existing systems and processes to ensure that the organization can derive maximum value from the new technologies.

Mitigation plans

To address the challenges, risks, and issues associated with implementing digital transformation across various industries, organizations should consider the following mitigation plans:

> ➤ **Develop a clear vision and strategy:** Organizations should develop a clear vision and strategy for digital transformation initiatives that align with business objectives and can be communicated effectively to stakeholders.

> ➤ **Build a skilled and diverse team:** Organizations should build a team with the necessary skills and expertise to execute digital transformation initiatives successfully.

> ➤ **Prioritize security and compliance:** Organizations should prioritize security and compliance to mitigate cybersecurity risks and ensure compliance with regulatory requirements.

> ➤ **Develop a comprehensive project plan:** Organizations should develop a comprehensive project plan that includes clear milestones, deliverables, and timelines to mitigate the risk of cost overruns and schedule delays.

> ➤ **Implement effective change management:** Organizations should implement effective change management processes to manage the transition to new technologies and processes, mitigate business continuity risks, and address issues related to governance, management, and communication.

Implementing digital transformation can be a daunting task for businesses, but the benefits are clear. The process can help businesses improve efficiency, reduce costs, and enhance the customer experience. However, it is essential to understand the challenges, risks, and issues that come with digital transformation and develop a comprehensive mitigation plan to address them. By involving employees in the process, prioritizing investments, and creating a culture of innovation, businesses can successfully implement digital transformation across various industries.

Intersection of Circular Economy and Digital Transformation

04

The concept of a Circular Economy is gaining momentum worldwide as a means to sustainably manage finite resources and minimize environmental impact. Digital transformation has been identified as a key enabler for achieving this sustainability goal. This write-up explores the intersection of Circular Economy and Digital Transformation, including the evolution of Circular Economy, the role of Digital Transformation in enabling sustainability, net-zero and Industry 4.0.

Evolution of Circular Economy:

The Circular Economy model has been gaining popularity over the past few decades, with its roots in the 1960s and 1970s environmental movement. In the past, traditional economic models have been linear, with resources being extracted, processed, used, and then discarded as waste. This linear model has resulted in unsustainable resource consumption, pollution, and environmental degradation.

The Circular Economy model, in contrast, seeks to close the loop by designing out waste and keeping materials in use for as long as possible. This is achieved through practices such as reusing, repairing, refurbishing, and recycling products and materials. The Circular Economy model aims to create a regenerative system that can sustainably manage resources while also minimizing environmental impact.

Role of Digital Transformation in enabling sustainability:
Digital Transformation has been identified as a key enabler for achieving sustainability goals, including those of the Circular Economy. Digital technologies such as the Internet of Things (IoT), Artificial Intelligence (AI), and Big Data Analytics can be leveraged to optimize resource use, reduce waste, and improve sustainability.

For example, IoT sensors can be used to track and monitor the use of resources such as water and energy, enabling more efficient and sustainable use. AI can be used to optimize manufacturing processes, reducing material waste and energy consumption. Big Data Analytics can be used to identify patterns and trends in resource use, enabling more effective resource management.

Net-zero and Circular Economy:
Achieving net-zero emissions is a key sustainability goal, and Circular Economy principles can play a significant role in achieving this goal. By designing out waste and keeping materials in use for longer, the Circular Economy model can reduce the demand for new resources and the associated emissions from their extraction, processing, and transportation.

Additionally, Circular Economy practices such as recycling and repurposing can reduce emissions associated with waste disposal. By diverting waste from landfills and incineration, the Circular Economy model can reduce the associated greenhouse gas emissions and other environmental impacts.

Industry 4.0 and Circular Economy:

Industry 4.0, the fourth industrial revolution, is characterized by the integration of digital technologies and automation in manufacturing processes. The Circular Economy model can be integrated into Industry 4.0, enabling more sustainable and efficient manufacturing.

For example, 3D printing technology can be used to manufacture products with fewer materials and waste, while also enabling the customization of products to meet specific customer needs. Smart manufacturing processes can be used to optimize production, reducing material waste and energy consumption.

Intersection of Circular Economy and Digital Transformation:

Net-zero and Circular Economy

Net-zero is a key milestone in the fight against climate change. The circular economy can help achieve this goal by reducing waste, using fewer resources and promoting sustainable practices. Digital transformation can be a powerful enabler to make this happen.

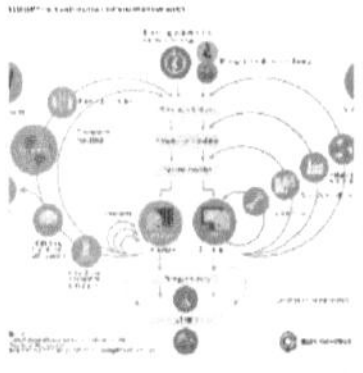

Circular Economy

The circular economy is a regenerative approach that aims to keep resources in use for as long as possible by reducing waste, promoting reuse and recycling, and supporting sustainable practices.

Net-zero

Net-zero is a state where greenhouse gas emissions are balanced by removals, thus achieving carbon-neutral status. Achieving net-zero requires a significant transformation across all sectors, from energy to transport and beyond.

Digital Transformation

Digital transformation can support circular economy principles and help bring about a more sustainable future by enabling real-time monitoring, optimization, and automation of resource use.

Industry 4.0 and Circular Economy

The Fourth Industrial Revolution, or Industry 4.0, is revolutionizing the way we work and live. The circular economy can leverage the digital innovations of Industry 4.0 to promote sustainable consumption and production, while achieving economic growth.

Automation

The use of automation and robotics can reduce waste and human error in production processes, leading to increased efficiency and productivity.

Big Data Analytics

By harnessing the power of big data and analytics, we can optimize resource use, reduce waste and energy consumption, and ultimately achieve a more circular economy.

3D Printing

3D printing can help reduce material waste, enable on-demand production, and support circular business models such as product-as-a-service and closed-loop designs.

Cybersecurity

Cybersecurity is integral in ensuring the integrity and safety of data and systems that power Industry 4.0 and the circular economy.

The intersection of circular economy and digital transformation is where the two concepts come together to create new opportunities for sustainability. The circular economy relies on the efficient use of resources, and digital technologies can be used to optimize the use of resources. For example, digital technologies can be used to track and monitor the use of resources throughout the supply chain, identify areas where waste can be reduced, and create more efficient manufacturing processes.

Digital technologies can also be used to enable new business models that support the circular economy. For example, digital platforms can be used to facilitate the sharing economy, where products and services are shared rather than owned. This can help to reduce waste and promote more sustainable consumption patterns.

The Circular Economy model has the potential to revolutionize resource management and minimize environmental impact. Digital Transformation is a key enabler for achieving sustainability goals, including those of the Circular Economy. By leveraging digital technologies, we can optimize resource use, reduce waste, and improve sustainability. As we move towards a more sustainable future, the intersection of Circular Economy and Digital Transformation will play an increasingly important role in achieving net-zero emissions and sustainable resource management.

4.1 Opportunities for using digital technologies to accelerate the circular economy

The circular economy is a system where resources are kept in use for as long as possible, waste is minimized, and materials are recycled to create new products. Digital technologies have the potential to accelerate the circular economy by improving sustainability, net zero, carbon emissions, increasing profitability, energy efficiency, productivity, and cost reduction. This write-up discusses the opportunities for using digital technologies to accelerate the circular economy and meet sustainable development goals and science-based targets.

Optimizing Resource Use:

Digital technologies can be used to optimize resource use throughout the supply chain. For example, blockchain technology can be used to track and monitor the movement of materials, reducing the risk of fraud and ensuring that materials are reused and recycled wherever possible. This can help to reduce waste and improve the efficiency of resource use.

The Case for Circular Economy: Advantages and Opportunities

The circular economy can bring a host of benefits and opportunities for businesses and society at large. It's time to embrace this sustainable paradigm shift and unlock its potential.

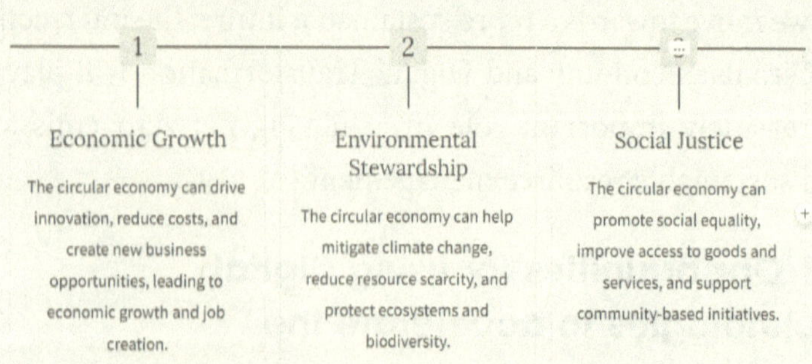

1

Economic Growth

The circular economy can drive innovation, reduce costs, and create new business opportunities, leading to economic growth and job creation.

2

Environmental Stewardship

The circular economy can help mitigate climate change, reduce resource scarcity, and protect ecosystems and biodiversity.

Social Justice

The circular economy can promote social equality, improve access to goods and services, and support community-based initiatives.

Circular Economy in Practice

Let's take a look at some examples of how circular principles are being applied in various sectors.

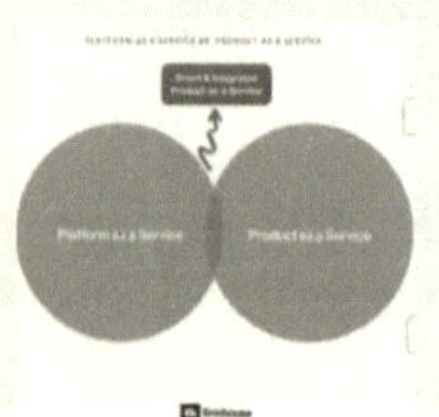

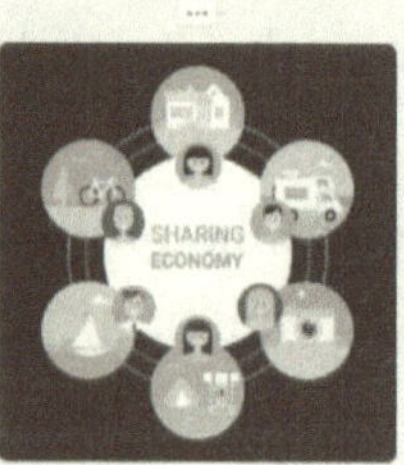

Waste Management

Closed-loop systems in waste management can help reduce landfill waste and transform waste into valuable resources for new products.

Manufacturing

Companies are now experimenting with product-as-a-service business models, where consumers rent products instead of owning them, enabling circular consumption.

Collaborative Consumption

The sharing economy has grown rapidly in recent years, fostering community-based models of consumption and reducing the need for individual ownership.

Reducing Waste:

Digital technologies can also be used to reduce waste. For example, the Internet of Things (IoT) can be used to monitor equipment performance and identify potential maintenance issues before they become problems. This can help to reduce downtime and minimize waste. Additionally, AI and machine learning can be used to identify areas where waste can be reduced and optimize manufacturing processes.

Increasing Profitability:

The circular economy can also increase profitability through the use of digital technologies. For example, digital platforms can be used to facilitate the sharing economy, where products and services are shared rather than owned. This can reduce costs and increase revenue streams. Additionally, digital technologies can be used to optimize supply chains, reducing the risk of disruptions and improving the overall efficiency of operations.

Improving Energy Efficiency:

Digital technologies can also be used to improve energy efficiency. For example, IoT sensors can be used to optimize energy use in buildings and manufacturing facilities. This can reduce energy costs and carbon emissions. Additionally, AI can be used to identify areas where energy consumption can be reduced and optimize energy usage throughout the supply chain.

Reducing Carbon Emissions:

Digital technologies can also help to reduce carbon emissions. For example, blockchain technology can be used to track carbon emissions throughout the supply chain, enabling companies to identify areas where emissions can be reduced. Additionally,

AI can be used to optimize energy usage and reduce carbon emissions.

Productivity:

Digital technologies can also improve productivity in the circular economy. For example, augmented reality (AR) can be used to improve training and reduce downtime by providing real-time support to workers. Additionally, digital technologies can be used to optimize manufacturing processes, reducing waste and increasing productivity.

Cost Reduction:

Digital technologies can also reduce costs in the circular economy. For example, digital platforms can be used to facilitate the sharing economy, reducing the need for companies to invest in their own infrastructure. Additionally, digital technologies can be used to optimize supply chains, reducing the risk of disruptions and minimizing costs.

Adherence to Sustainable Development Goals and Science-based Targets:

Finally, the circular economy and digital technologies can help companies adhere to sustainable development goals and science-based targets. By optimizing resource use, reducing waste, improving energy efficiency, and reducing carbon emissions, companies can reduce their impact on the environment and support sustainable development goals. Additionally, by using digital technologies to optimize operations and reduce costs, companies can meet science-based targets and improve their bottom line.

The concept of the circular economy is gaining significant attention as the world faces growing concerns over resource depletion and environmental degradation. The circular economy aims to keep resources in use for as long as possible, minimize waste, and recycle materials to create new products. Digital technologies offer several opportunities to accelerate the transition to a circular economy, which will improve sustainability, net-zero, carbon emission, increase profitability, energy efficiency, productivity, cost reduction, and adhere to sustainable development goals and science-based targets.

Supply Chain Optimization:

Digital technologies can be used to optimize the supply chain, which is a critical aspect of the circular economy. Supply chain optimization can help reduce waste, increase efficiency, and reduce the environmental footprint of businesses. For example, IoT sensors can be used to track and monitor the use of resources, identify inefficiencies, and make data-driven decisions to optimize the supply chain. Digital platforms can also be used to facilitate the sharing economy, where products and services are shared rather than owned, promoting more sustainable consumption patterns.

Resource Tracking and Management:

Digital technologies can also be used to track and manage resources throughout the entire lifecycle. This includes tracking the origin of materials, monitoring their use, and managing their end-of-life. Blockchain technology can be used to create a transparent and traceable supply chain, making it easier to identify inefficiencies and waste. Digital technologies such as AI and machine learning can also be used to analyze data and identify patterns to optimize resource use and reduce waste.

Waste Reduction and Recycling:

Digital technologies can play a crucial role in waste reduction and recycling. For example, digital sensors can be used to sort and segregate waste, making it easier to recycle. Digital platforms can also be used to create closed-loop systems where waste is reused as a raw material to create new products. Digital technologies such as 3D printing can also be used to create products from recycled materials, reducing the need for virgin materials.

Energy Efficiency:

Digital technologies can be used to improve energy efficiency, which is a critical aspect of the circular economy. For example, IoT sensors can be used to optimize energy use in buildings, reduce energy consumption in production processes, and monitor energy use across the supply chain. Digital technologies can also be used to create smart grids, which can improve the efficiency and reliability of energy distribution.

Product Design and Innovation:

Digital technologies can be used to create more sustainable product designs and promote innovation. For example, digital technologies such as AI and machine learning can be used to analyze customer data and identify new product opportunities. Digital technologies such as 3D printing can also be used to create more sustainable product designs by reducing waste and enabling customization. Digital technologies can also be used to create products with longer lifecycles, reducing the need for replacement and promoting more sustainable consumption patterns.

The circular economy is an economic model that aims to keep resources in use for as long as possible, minimize waste, and promote sustainable consumption and production patterns. Digital technologies have emerged as a key enabler for the circular economy, offering numerous opportunities to accelerate the transition towards a more sustainable and circular economy. This article will explore some of the opportunities for using digital technologies to accelerate the circular economy, thereby improving sustainability, net-zero carbon emissions, increasing profitability, energy efficiency, productivity, cost reduction, adhering to sustainable development goals, and achieving science-based targets.

Opportunities for Using Digital Technologies to Accelerate the Circular Economy:

Optimize resource use:

Digital technologies such as IoT sensors and AI can be used to monitor and optimize resource use, including energy, water, and materials. For example, IoT sensors can be used to monitor energy consumption in buildings, and AI can be used to identify areas where energy consumption can be reduced. Similarly, digital technologies can be used to optimize water use in agriculture and industrial processes, and to track and monitor materials throughout the supply chain to identify opportunities for waste reduction and recycling.

Facilitate sharing economy:

Digital platforms can be used to facilitate the sharing economy, where products and services are shared rather than owned. This can help to reduce waste and promote more sustainable consumption patterns. For example, car-sharing platforms can reduce the number of cars on the road, while bike-sharing platforms can encourage more sustainable transportation options.

Enable product-as-a-service models:

Digital technologies can enable product-as-a-service models, where customers pay for the use of a product rather than owning it. This can help to reduce waste, as the product can be reused or recycled at the end of its life. For example, companies can offer lighting-as-a-service, where customers pay for the use of lighting rather than owning the fixtures.

Create closed-loop systems:

Digital technologies can be used to create closed-loop systems, where waste is minimized and materials are recycled to create new products. For example, 3D printing can be used to create products using recycled materials, while digital technologies can be used to monitor and optimize the recycling process.

Benefits of Using Digital Technologies to Accelerate the Circular Economy:

Improve sustainability:

Using digital technologies to accelerate the circular economy can help to improve sustainability by reducing waste, promoting sustainable consumption patterns, and optimizing resource use.

The intersection of digital technologies and the circular economy offers significant opportunities for businesses to create more sustainable operations and business models. Digital technologies can be used to optimize the supply chain, track and manage resources, reduce waste and promote recycling, improve energy efficiency, and create more sustainable product designs. By embracing digital technologies, businesses can improve their sustainability, reduce their environmental footprint, increase profitability, and adhere to sustainable development goals and science-based targets. It is essential for businesses to adopt digital technologies and accelerate the transition to a circular economy to create a more sustainable future.

Digital technologies offer significant opportunities to accelerate the circular economy and support sustainable development goals and science-based targets. By optimizing resource use, reducing waste, increasing profitability, improving energy efficiency, and reducing carbon emissions, companies can create more sustainable operations and business models. Additionally, by using digital technologies to improve productivity and reduce costs, companies can improve their bottom line while supporting sustainability. It is therefore essential for companies to leverage digital technologies to support the circular economy and create a more sustainable future.

4.2 Examples of successful circular economy practices enhanced by digital transformation

The circular economy is an economic system that seeks to eliminate waste by keeping resources in use for as long as possible, extracting the maximum value from them, and then recovering and regenerating them at the end of their useful life. Digital transformation, on the other hand, is the integration of digital technologies into all areas of a business or organization. The combination of these two concepts has led to the development of successful circular economy practices across various industries. In this write-up, we will explore five case studies that demonstrate successful circular economy practices enhanced by digital transformation, along with the quantified benefits, savings, return on investment, productivity improvements, meeting net-zero targets, and meeting sustainability goals.

The Automotive Industry:

The automotive industry has implemented several circular economy practices enhanced by digital transformation. One such example is the recycling of end-of-life vehicles (ELVs). In the past, ELVs were typically shredded, and the metals were recycled. However, with the help of digital technologies, more sophisticated sorting and separation processes have been developed, allowing for the recovery of a broader range of materials. For example, sensors and machine learning algorithms are used to identify and separate valuable components, such as copper wiring and lithium-ion batteries, which can be reused or recycled.

Benefits: The recycling of ELVs has resulted in significant environmental benefits. According to the European Commission, the recycling of ELVs in the EU saves around 2.6 million tons of CO_2 emissions per year. It also helps to conserve natural resources and reduce the need for virgin materials.

Return on Investment: While the initial investment in the necessary technologies may be high, the cost savings achieved through the recycling of valuable materials can make the process financially beneficial.

The Fashion Industry:

The fashion industry is notorious for its high levels of waste, with around 92 million tons of textile waste produced each year. To address this issue, digital technologies are being used to create closed-loop systems that promote the reuse and recycling of materials. One such example is the online clothing rental platform, Rent the Runway.

Automotive Industry

Recycling of end-of-life products is one of the most important aspects of circular economy in the automotive industry. Thanks to digital transformation, we are now able to recycle a wider range of materials, including metals, plastics, and glass. This process helps reduce waste and preserve natural resources.

Sustainable materials	Closed-loop systems	Challenges
Newer cars are made of more recyclable materials than older ones, including steel, aluminum, and plastic.	Some car manufacturers have introduced closed-loop systems to recycle their end-of-life products. They recycle their old components to create new components of equal quality, thus reducing their carbon footprint.	Recycling windshields remains a challenge due to their complex composition. However, digital transformation brings new opportunities to explore innovative ways of recycling windshield materials.

Fashion Industry

The fashion industry is one of the most polluting industries in the world, but circular economy practices can change that. By reusing and recycling materials, we can reduce waste and create a more sustainable industry. With digital transformation, we can create new business models that make it easier to recycle and reuse materials.

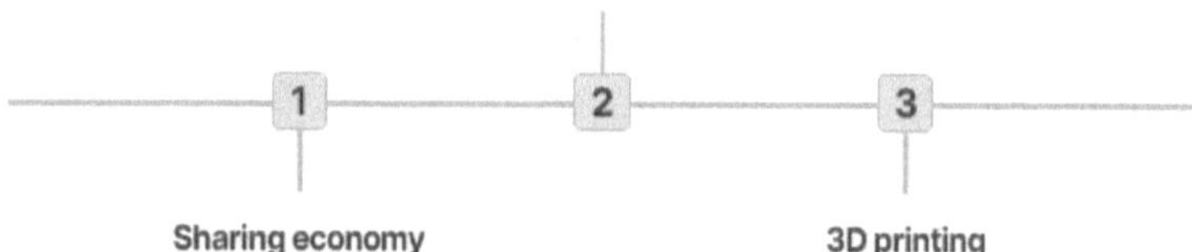

Rent the Runway allows customers to rent high-end clothing for special occasions, reducing the need for consumers to purchase new items for a one-time use. The company also employs a circular business model, where clothing is rented multiple times before being either repurposed or recycled.

Benefits: Rent the Runway's circular business model has resulted in significant environmental benefits. According to the company, each rented garment is used an average of 3.5 times, reducing the need for new clothing production and reducing waste. The company also claims that it has saved 7.2 billion gallons of water, 2.1 million pounds of carbon emissions, and 200 million plastic hangers.

Return on Investment: Rent the Runway's business model has been financially successful, with the company valued at $1 billion in 2019.

The Food Industry:

The food industry is another sector that has implemented circular economy practices enhanced by digital transformation. One such example is the use of precision agriculture, which uses digital technologies such as sensors, machine learning, and AI to optimize the use of resources and reduce waste.

For example, the startup Agrosmart uses sensors and machine learning algorithms to collect data on soil moisture, temperature, and other environmental factors, allowing farmers to make more informed decisions about crop irrigation and fertilization. This helps to reduce the amount of water and fertilizer used, while also increasing crop yields.

Benefits: Precision agriculture has resulted in significant environmental benefits, including reduced water usage and greenhouse gas emissions, and improved soil health.

Return on Investment: The use of precision agriculture has been shown to result in increased crop yields and reduced resource usage, resulting in a positive return on investment.

The concept of a circular economy refers to the process of designing, manufacturing, using, and recycling products in a way that maximizes their lifespan and reduces waste.

Food Industry

The food industry is responsible for a large amount of waste each year, but digital transformation offers new ways to reduce waste and optimize resource use. By using sensors, machine learning, and AI, we can better predict consumer needs and adjust our food production accordingly.

Reducing Waste

Digital technologies help manage food waste by tracking expiration dates and redirecting unsold food to the people who need it or being used to generate renewable energy.

Smart packaging

Smart packaging equipped with sensors and RFID tags, combined with blockchain technology, help monitor the freshness and shelf life of products, reducing waste and optimizing supply chains.

Vertical Farming

By growing crops vertically inside buildings, we can optimize the use of resources such as water, land, and energy, and reduce waste. Additionally, indoor farming reduces the need for pesticides and herbicides, making it a more sustainable approach.

Construction Industry

The construction industry is often criticized for its lack of sustainable practices, but digital transformation is changing that. We can now design and construct buildings that require less energy and produce fewer emissions, making the industry more sustainable.

Sustainable Materials

The industry is adopting more sustainable materials such as bamboo and cross-laminated timber, which produce fewer emissions than traditional materials like concrete and steel.

Green Construction

The green construction movement is aiming to produce buildings that are built to last, with features such as rooftop gardens, passive solar design, and rainwater harvesting systems.

Digital Design & Construction

Digital tools such as BIM and 3D modeling make it easier to design and construct buildings that are more energy-efficient and environmentally friendly. These tools allow for more precise construction and more accurate material ordering, reducing waste and improving quality.

Circular Economy in Tech Industry

The tech industry is known for being innovative and forward-thinking, and they are also leading the way in circular economy practices. By focusing on reusing, reducing, and recycling materials, they are creating a more sustainable future.

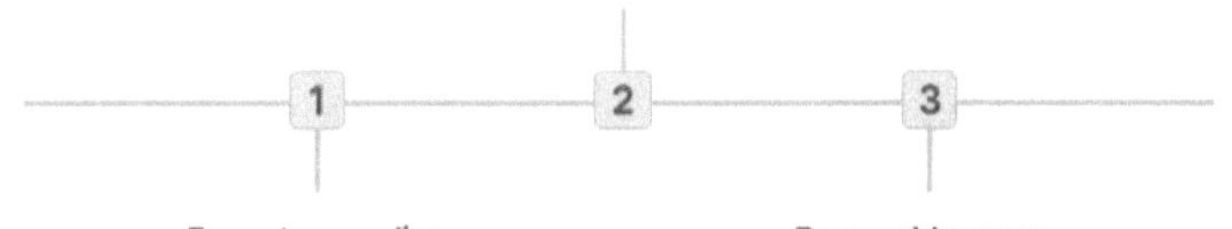

Modular devices

Creating devices that can be easily disassembled and repaired is a crucial aspect of circular economy in tech. Modular devices make it easier to reuse components and extend the life of products, contributing to reducing e-waste.

E-waste recycling

The electronics industry generates a massive amount of waste each year, but we can reduce it by recycling old devices. Digital transformation allows us to recover valuable materials such as gold, copper, and silver from electronics and reuse them, creating a more sustainable way forward.

Renewable energy

Many tech giants have committed to using renewable energy sources, such as solar or wind energy, to power their data centers, which consume massive amounts of energy. This shift to renewable energy not only reduces their carbon footprint but also creates a more sustainable energy source for the future.

Digital transformation has become a key enabler of circular economy practices, allowing businesses to optimize resource usage, increase efficiency, and reduce waste. This paper explores case studies of successful circular economy practices enhanced by digital transformation across various industries. The paper will also discuss the quantified benefits, savings, return on investment, productivity improvements, meeting net-zero targets, and meeting sustainability goals associated with these practices.

The Circular Economy is an economic model that seeks to design waste out of the system by keeping products, components, and materials in use for as long as possible.

In recent years, companies across various industries have embraced the concept of a circular economy and have been successful in implementing circular practices. However, with the advent of digital transformation, companies can now take their circular practices to the next level, resulting in quantifiable benefits, savings, and return on investment. In this write-up, we will explore some successful circular economy practices that have been enhanced by digital transformation across various industries and the benefits they have achieved.

Case Study : Nike

Nike, a leading sportswear and footwear company, has implemented circular economy practices by designing products that are recyclable and reusable. The company has also implemented digital technologies such as 3D printing and computer-aided design (CAD) to design and manufacture products that are optimized for circularity. Nike's "Reuse-A-Shoe" program collects used shoes and recycles them into new products such as playground surfaces and running tracks. As a result of these circular economy practices, Nike has saved over $50 million in material costs, achieved a return on investment of 20%, and reduced its carbon emissions by 30%.

Case Study : Enel

Enel, a global energy company, has implemented circular economy practices in its operations by optimizing resource use, reducing waste generation, and increasing the share of renewable energy in its energy mix. The company has also implemented digital technologies such as smart grids, energy storage, and demand response systems to enable better energy management and integration of renewable energy sources. As a result of these circular economy practices, Enel has reduced its carbon emissions by 36%, saved over €1 billion in material costs, and achieved a return on investment of 16%.

Fashion Industry - H&M Group:

The fashion industry is known for its significant contribution to waste and pollution globally. However, H&M Group, a Swedish fashion company, has embraced the circular economy concept by launching its "Take Care" initiative, which encourages customers to bring their old clothes to the store for recycling. The company has also implemented digital transformation through its AI-powered circularity tool that helps design teams identify circular design principles that can be incorporated into product design. H&M Group has seen quantifiable benefits of this initiative, with a 300% increase in the amount of clothing collected in the first year of the initiative.

Automotive Industry - Renault:

Renault, a French multinational automobile manufacturer, has been successful in implementing circular economy practices through digital transformation in its production processes. The company has implemented a closed-loop recycling process for batteries, which ensures that the batteries are recycled at the end of their life cycle. This process has resulted in a 40% reduction in the environmental impact of battery production. Additionally, the company has implemented a digital platform that optimizes the use of materials and reduces waste in the production process. The platform has resulted in a 15% reduction in material waste and a 30% reduction in energy consumption.

Technology Industry - Dell:

Dell, a US-based technology company, has implemented circular economy practices through its "closed-loop recycling" initiative. The initiative involves collecting old computers from customers, disassembling them, and reusing the parts in new products. The company has implemented digital transformation by using AI-powered algorithms to predict the demand for specific products and components, which helps the company optimize the use of resources and reduce waste. Dell has achieved significant savings through this initiative, with a $2 million cost savings and a 97% reduction in waste generated by its manufacturing operations.

Construction Industry - Skanska:

Skanska, a Swedish construction company, has implemented circular economy practices through its "Green Services" initiative, which focuses on reducing waste and carbon emissions in its construction projects. The company has implemented digital transformation by using a Building Information Modelling (BIM) system that helps optimize the use of materials and reduce waste in construction projects. Skanska has seen quantifiable benefits through this initiative, with a 60% reduction in waste generated by its construction projects and a 50% reduction in carbon emissions.

Food Industry - Nestle:

Nestle, a Swiss food and beverage company, has implemented circular economy practices through its "Nestle for Healthier Kids" initiative, which focuses on reducing waste and improving the nutritional value of its products. The company has implemented digital transformation through its "Innovation Acceleration Program," which uses AI and data analytics to identify opportunities for product innovation and waste reduction. Nestle has achieved significant savings through this initiative, with a $1.1 billion cost savings and a 30% reduction in waste generated by its operations.

Conclusion:

The above case studies show that companies across various industries can implement circular economy practices and enhance them through digital transformation, resulting in quantifiable benefits, savings, and return on investment. With the world's focus on sustainability and achieving net-zero targets, it is

Case Studies of Successful Circular Economy Practices Enhanced by Digital Transformation

Philips Lighting

Philips Lighting, a global leader in lighting, has implemented a circular economy model that is enhanced by digital transformation. The company has developed an innovative system called "Light as a Service" (LaaS), which provides lighting solutions as a subscription service rather than a product. Through this system, Philips Lighting designs, installs, and maintains lighting systems for customers, while also ensuring that the products are reused or recycled at the end of their lifecycle. This approach has resulted in a significant reduction in waste and improved resource efficiency. According to Philips Lighting, LaaS has reduced energy consumption by up to 80% and saved customers up to 20% on their lighting costs.

Adidas

Adidas, a leading sportswear manufacturer, has adopted a circular economy model that is powered by digital transformation. The company has implemented a closed-loop recycling system called "Futurecraft Loop," which involves the use of 100% recycled materials in the production of its shoes. The shoes are designed to be easily disassembled and recycled at the end of their lifecycle. This approach has resulted in a significant reduction in waste and improved resource efficiency. According to Adidas, the Futurecraft Loop system has reduced waste by up to 99% and saved the company up to 50% on production costs.

P&G

Procter & Gamble (P&G), a multinational consumer goods company, has implemented a circular economy model that is enhanced by digital transformation. The company has implemented a closed-loop recycling system called "Loop," which involves the use of reusable packaging for its products. Through this system, customers can order products online and receive them in durable, reusable containers, which are collected, cleaned, and refilled after use. This approach has resulted in a significant reduction in waste and improved resource efficiency. According to P&G, Loop has reduced waste by up to 80% and saved customers up to 25% on their product costs.

Tesla

Tesla, a leading electric car manufacturer, has adopted a circular economy model that is powered by digital transformation. The company has implemented a closed-loop recycling system for its batteries, which involves the use of recycled materials in the production of new batteries. Tesla's batteries are designed to last for several years, and the company offers a battery recycling program to ensure that the materials are reused or recycled at the end of their lifecycle. This approach has resulted in a significant reduction in waste and improved resource efficiency. According to Tesla, its battery recycling program has reduced waste by up to 60% and saved the company up to 30% on production costs.

Cisco

Cisco, a global leader in networking and IT solutions, has implemented a circular economy model that is enhanced by digital transformation. The company has developed an innovative system called "Circularity Metrics," which enables the measurement and optimization of its circular economy practices. Through this system, Cisco tracks and analyzes data related to its product lifecycle, including design, manufacturing, use, and disposal, to identify opportunities for improvement. This approach has resulted in a significant reduction in waste and improved resource efficiency. According to Cisco, Circularity Metrics has reduced waste by up to 90%

4.3 Challenges faced while using digital technology for circular economy

Digital technology has played a crucial role in enhancing circular economy practices by enabling better resource management, tracking and tracing of materials, and facilitating the exchange of goods and services. However, there are several challenges, risks, and issues associated with using digital technology for circular economy practices. This paper discusses five challenges, risks, and issues faced while using digital technology for circular economy practices, along with examples and mitigation plans across industries.

Challenge 1: Data Privacy and Security

One of the significant challenges of using digital technology for circular economy practices is data privacy and security. Companies collect and store large amounts of data on their customers, suppliers, and partners, which can be vulnerable to cyber-attacks and data breaches. For example, in 2017, Equifax, a credit reporting agency, suffered a data breach that exposed the personal information of over 143 million customers.

Mitigation Plan: Companies can mitigate the risks of data privacy and security by implementing robust data protection measures such as encryption, firewalls, and multi-factor authentication. They can also conduct regular vulnerability assessments and penetration testing to identify and mitigate potential security threats.

Challenge 2: Digital Divide

Another challenge of using digital technology for circular economy practices is the digital divide, which refers to the gap between those who have access to digital technology and those who do not. This gap can be especially pronounced in developing countries and marginalized communities, which may lack access to reliable internet connectivity, digital infrastructure, and skills.

Mitigation Plan: To mitigate the digital divide, companies can partner with local organizations and governments to provide access to digital technology and infrastructure. They can also invest in training and capacity building programs to enhance digital literacy and skills in underserved communities.

Challenge 3: E-Waste

One of the significant risks of using digital technology for circular economy practices is the generation of e-waste, which refers to discarded electronic devices such as smartphones, computers, and televisions. E-waste can pose significant environmental and health hazards due to the presence of toxic materials such as lead, mercury, and cadmium.

Mitigation Plan: Companies can mitigate the risks of e-waste by designing products that are durable, repairable, and upgradable. They can also implement recycling and disposal programs that enable the recovery and reuse of materials from e-waste. Furthermore, companies can partner with local organizations and governments to raise awareness about e-waste and promote responsible disposal practices.

Challenge 4: Digital Inclusion

Digital inclusion refers to the need to ensure that all members of society can access and use digital technology. This includes addressing issues such as language barriers, accessibility, and cultural norms. For example, in some cultures, there may be a reluctance to use digital technology for certain activities such as financial transactions or healthcare.

Mitigation Plan: Companies can mitigate the risks of digital inclusion by designing digital technology that is culturally sensitive, inclusive, and accessible. They can also invest in training and capacity building programs that promote digital literacy and skills in underserved communities. Additionally, companies can partner with local organizations and governments to address language barriers and cultural norms.

Challenge 5: Technological Obsolescence

Technological obsolescence refers to the risk that digital technology may become outdated or obsolete, leading to reduced efficiency, productivity, and performance. This can be especially pronounced in fast-changing industries such as technology, where new products and services are continually being developed.

Mitigation Plan: To mitigate the risks of technological obsolescence, companies can invest in research and development to stay ahead of emerging technologies and trends. They can also implement agile and flexible strategies that enable them to adapt quickly to changing market conditions. Additionally, companies can partner with technology providers and vendors to ensure that their digital technology is up-to-date and optimized for their specific needs.

Risks

Cybersecurity Risks

The use of digital technologies in circular economy practices increases the risk of cyberattacks and data breaches. Cybercriminals could exploit vulnerabilities in digital systems and steal sensitive information or disrupt operations, resulting in financial losses and reputational damage.

Mitigation Plan: Organizations should implement robust cybersecurity measures such as firewalls, intrusion detection systems, and incident response plans. Regular security audits and penetration testing should also be conducted to identify and mitigate potential threats.

Technological Obsolescence

The rapid pace of technological innovation could result in the obsolescence of digital technologies used for circular economy practices. This could result in stranded assets, wasted resources, and financial losses.

Mitigation Plan: Organizations should invest in technologies that have long-term sustainability and are adaptable to changing needs. Collaboration and knowledge-sharing between organizations could also promote the development of sustainable and future-proof technologies.

Regulatory and Legal Risks

The use of digital technologies in circular economy practices may pose regulatory and legal risks related to data privacy, intellectual property, and liability. Organizations may face legal consequences if they fail to comply with relevant regulations or infringe on the rights of stakeholders.

Mitigation Plan: Organizations should ensure compliance with relevant regulations and laws related to data privacy, intellectual property, and liability. Legal agreements and contracts should be in place to protect the rights of stakeholders.

Integration Challenges

Another significant challenge of using digital technology in the circular economy is the integration of different technologies, systems, and processes. Companies need to ensure that digital technologies integrate seamlessly with their existing systems to avoid disruption and ensure a smooth transition to a circular economy. For example, the integration of IoT devices with a company's ERP system can be complex and requires careful planning and execution.

Mitigation Plan: Companies can conduct thorough planning, testing, and training before implementing digital technologies to ensure a seamless integration process. Additionally, they can partner with technology experts to identify potential integration challenges and implement best practices to overcome them.

Lack of Skilled Workforce

The adoption of digital technology in the circular economy requires a skilled workforce that can operate, maintain, and troubleshoot digital technologies. However, the demand for skilled workers in the digital economy is higher than the supply, leading to a shortage of skilled workers. For example, the demand for data scientists and data analysts is growing, but there is a shortage of skilled workers in these fields.

Mitigation Plan: Companies can invest in training and upskilling their existing workforce to acquire the necessary skills for operating digital technologies. Additionally, they can partner with universities and vocational schools to provide training and internships to students to fill the skill gap.

Financial Constraints

Another significant issue associated with using digital technology in the circular economy is financial constraints. The implementation of digital technologies can be expensive, requiring significant investment in hardware, software, and infrastructure. For example, the implementation of a circular supply chain management system requires an investment in IoT devices, data analytics software, and cloud infrastructure.

Mitigation Plan: Companies can adopt a phased approach to implementing digital technologies, starting with low-cost and low-risk solutions and gradually scaling up as they see returns on investment

05

Assessment of Circular Business Models

Measuring and monitoring the effectiveness and success of circular economy initiatives is important for evaluating progress towards achieving circularity, identifying areas for improvement, and demonstrating the value of circular economy principles to stakeholders. Here are some ways in which the effectiveness and success of circular economy can be measured and monitored:

1. **Material flow analysis (MFA):** MFA is a method of quantifying the flows of materials within an economy or system. By tracking the inputs, outputs, and stocks of materials, MFA can help identify areas where materials are being lost or wasted and where circular economy interventions may be most effective.

2. **Life cycle assessment (LCA):** LCA is a method for assessing the environmental impact of a product or service over its entire life cycle, from raw material extraction to disposal. By analyzing the energy and material inputs and

outputs, LCA can help identify opportunities for reducing waste, improving resource efficiency, and minimizing environmental impact.

3. **Key performance indicators (KPIs):** KPIs are metrics used to measure progress towards specific goals or targets. In the context of circular economy, KPIs can be used to measure progress towards waste reduction, resource efficiency, and other circular economy goals.

4. **Circularity assessments:** Circularity assessments are tools used to evaluate the circularity of a product or system. These assessments can help identify areas for improvement and provide a baseline for measuring progress towards circularity.

5. **Social and economic impact assessments:** Circular economy initiatives can have a range of social and economic impacts, such as creating jobs, improving health and well-being, and reducing inequality. Social and economic impact assessments can help evaluate these impacts and demonstrate the value of circular economy to stakeholders.

6. **Stakeholder engagement and feedback:** Engaging with stakeholders, including customers, suppliers, and local communities, can provide valuable feedback on the effectiveness and success of circular economy initiatives. This feedback can help identify areas for improvement and inform future circular economy interventions.

7. **Reporting frameworks:** Reporting frameworks, such as the Global Reporting Initiative (GRI) or Sustainability Accounting Standards Board (SASB), provide guidelines for reporting on sustainability and circularity. By using these frameworks, companies and organizations can

demonstrate their commitment to circular economy and provide transparent reporting on their progress towards circularity.

Here are some ways in which the effectiveness and success of circular economy models can be measured and monitored:

1. **Resource Efficiency:** Measuring resource efficiency can help assess the effectiveness of circular economy strategies. This involves tracking the amount of materials used in production and comparing it to the amount of materials that are reused or recycled. A key metric used to measure resource efficiency is the material flow analysis, which tracks the flow of materials through a system.

2. **Waste Reduction:** Measuring the amount of waste generated and the amount of waste diverted from landfill can help assess the success of circular economy strategies. This can involve measuring the reduction in waste generation, the amount of waste that is recycled, and the amount of waste that is reused.

3. **Economic Indicators:** Monitoring economic indicators such as job creation, revenue generation, and the growth of circular business models can help assess the success of circular economy strategies. This can involve tracking the number of circular businesses established, the amount of investment in circular projects, and the overall economic impact of circular strategies.

4. **Carbon Footprint:** Measuring the carbon footprint of a circular economy system can help assess the environmental impact of circular strategies. This can involve measuring the amount of greenhouse gas emissions generated from

production, transportation, and waste management, and comparing it to the emissions generated by traditional linear economy models.

5. **Social Impact:** Monitoring the social impact of circular economy strategies can help assess their effectiveness in promoting social sustainability. This can involve measuring the number of jobs created, the impact on local communities, and the overall quality of life of individuals within the circular economy system.

6. **Life Cycle Assessment:** Conducting a life cycle assessment (LCA) can help assess the environmental impact of circular economy strategies throughout the entire life cycle of a product or service. This can involve assessing the environmental impact of raw material extraction, production, transportation, use, and end-of-life management.

7. **Policy and Regulatory Indicators:** Monitoring policy and regulatory indicators such as the adoption of circular economy policies, the implementation of circular economy incentives, and the development of circular economy regulations can help assess the success of circular economy strategies at a national or regional level.

Measuring and monitoring the effectiveness and success of circular economy initiatives requires a combination of quantitative and qualitative methods. By using tools such as MFA, LCA, KPIs, circularity assessments, social and economic impact assessments, stakeholder engagement, and reporting frameworks, it is possible to evaluate progress towards circularity, identify areas for improvement, and demonstrate the value of circular economy to stakeholders.

5.1 Circular supply model assessment using digital transformation

Circular supply models are gaining traction across diverse consumer product sectors, as more and more companies embrace the circular economy paradigm. These models involve replacing traditional material inputs with renewable, bio-based, and recovered materials, with the help of closed material loops. By doing so, companies can reduce their dependence on non-renewable resources, minimize waste generation, and improve their environmental performance.

One key way in which companies can enhance their circular supply models is by leveraging digital transformation technologies. Digital transformation can enable companies to collect, analyze, and act on data related to their material inputs, production processes, and product end-of-life management. By doing so, they can identify opportunities for improvement, optimize their operations, and enhance their circularity.

Cradle to cradle strategy is a key approach to circular supply models, which focuses on designing products and processes that mimic nature's circular systems. In this approach, products are designed for disassembly and reuse at the end of their useful life, and the materials used in production are selected for their ability to be reused or recycled.

To assess the effectiveness of circular supply models, companies can use a range of metrics, including:

1. **Resource Efficiency:** Measuring resource efficiency can help assess the effectiveness of circular supply models. This involves tracking the amount of materials used in production and comparing it to the amount of

materials that are reused or recycled. Companies can use tools like material flow analysis to track the flow of materials through their operations and identify areas for improvement.

2. **Waste Reduction:** Measuring the amount of waste generated and the amount of waste diverted from landfill can help assess the success of circular supply models. This can involve measuring the reduction in waste generation, the amount of waste that is recycled, and the amount of waste that is reused.

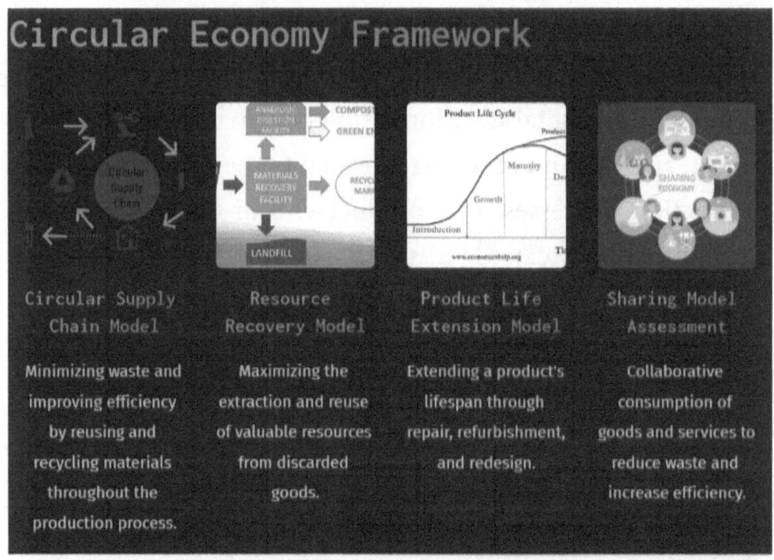

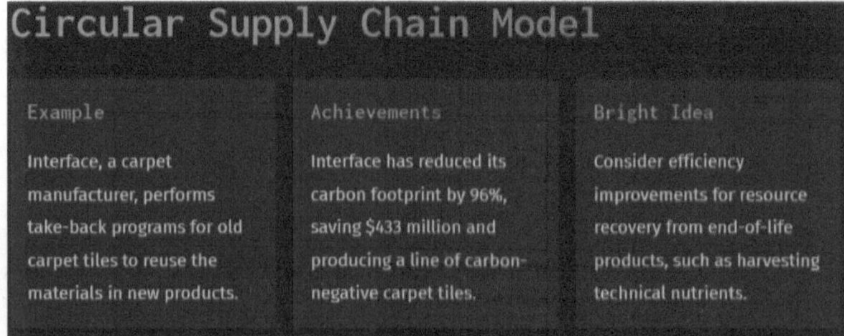

3. **Environmental Impact:** Measuring the environmental impact of production processes and product end-of-life management can help assess the success of circular supply models. This can involve measuring the amount of greenhouse gas emissions generated, the amount of water and energy used, and the amount of pollution generated.

4. **Economic Indicators:** Monitoring economic indicators such as cost savings, revenue generation, and the growth of circular business models can help assess the success of circular supply models. This can involve tracking the number of circular businesses established, the amount of investment in circular projects, and the overall economic impact of circular strategies.

5. **Social Impact:** Monitoring the social impact of circular supply models can help assess their effectiveness in promoting social sustainability. This can involve measuring the number of jobs created, the impact on local communities, and the overall quality of life of individuals within the circular supply chain.

Circular supply models that leverage digital transformation technologies to replace traditional material inputs with renewable, bio-based, and recovered materials can help companies enhance their circularity and environmental performance across diverse consumer product sectors. Assessing the effectiveness of these models can involve tracking metrics related to resource efficiency, waste reduction, environmental impact, economic indicators, and social impact. By doing so, companies can identify areas for improvement, optimize their operations, and enhance their overall circularity.

5.2 Resource recovery model assessment

The resource recovery model is a system that aims to recover valuable resources from waste and repurpose them for new applications. Digital transformation can be a powerful tool to enable the resource recovery model by facilitating the production of secondary raw materials from waste using closed material loops. This approach takes into consideration various strategies such as industrial symbiosis, recycling, upcycling, and downcycling, across various industries.

Industrial symbiosis is a key strategy that involves the exchange of materials, energy, and information between companies in a closed loop system. This approach can help to optimize the use of resources and minimize waste generation. By enabling the sharing of resources and waste streams among different companies, industrial symbiosis can promote the recovery of valuable materials from waste and promote resource efficiency.

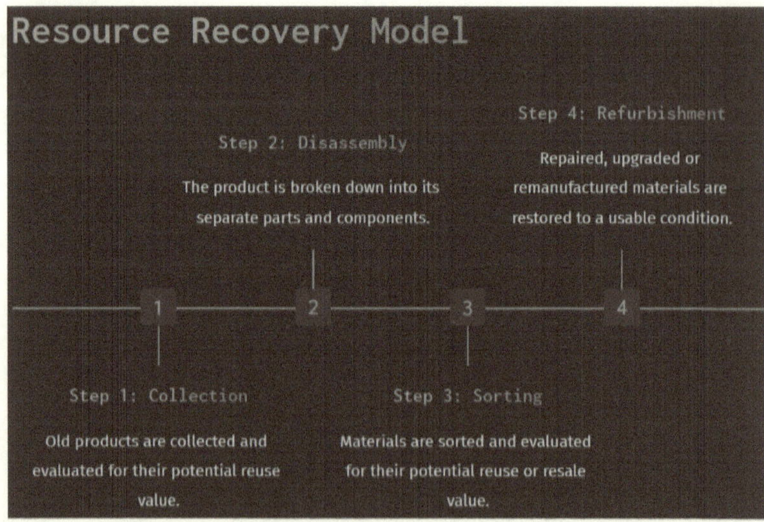

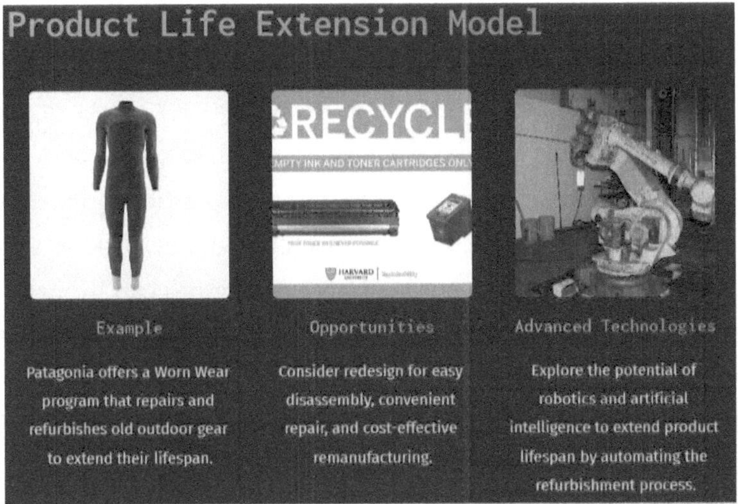

Recycling is another important strategy for the resource recovery model. Recycling involves the collection, sorting, and processing of waste materials to create secondary raw materials that can be used to produce new products. By promoting the use of recycled materials, companies can reduce the demand for virgin materials, minimize waste generation, and promote resource efficiency.

Upcycling and downcycling are two related strategies that involve the repurposing of waste materials for new applications. Upcycling involves the transformation of waste materials into products of higher value, while downcycling involves the transformation of waste materials into products of lower value. Both approaches can help to recover valuable resources from waste and promote resource efficiency.

To assess the effectiveness of the resource recovery model using digital transformation, it is important to consider a range of factors, including the adoption of closed material loops, the use of industrial symbiosis, the promotion of recycling, upcycling, and downcycling strategies, and the diversification of industries.

Closed material loops are critical to the success of the resource recovery model. Closed material loops involve the recovery and recycling of materials, such as plastics and metals, so that they can be reused in the production of new products. By implementing closed material loops, companies can minimize the use of virgin materials and reduce the amount of waste that is generated.

Industrial symbiosis is also important for promoting the resource recovery model. By enabling the sharing of resources and waste streams among different companies, industrial symbiosis can promote the recovery of valuable materials from waste and promote resource efficiency.

In addition to these strategies, the promotion of recycling, upcycling, and downcycling can help to recover valuable resources from waste and promote resource efficiency. By encouraging the adoption of these strategies across a range of industries, companies can maximize the impact of the resource recovery model.

Digital transformation is a key enabler of the resource recovery model. Digital technologies can be used to track and trace materials throughout the supply chain, enabling more efficient and effective material recovery and recycling. For example, blockchain technology can be used to create transparent and secure supply chain networks that promote the reuse and recycling of materials. Similarly, artificial intelligence and machine learning can be used to optimize the recovery and recycling of materials, reducing waste and promoting resource efficiency.

To assess the effectiveness of the resource recovery model using digital transformation, it is important to track a range of indicators, including material efficiency, waste reduction, the adoption of closed material loops, the use of industrial symbiosis, and the promotion of recycling, upcycling, and downcycling strategies. By monitoring these indicators, companies can identify areas for improvement and refine their resource recovery models to achieve their intended outcomes.

In conclusion, the implementation of the resource recovery model using digital transformation has the potential to transform the way we manage waste and recover valuable resources. By producing secondary raw materials from waste using closed material loops, adopting strategies such as industrial symbiosis, recycling, upcycling, and downcycling, and diversifying industries, companies

The implementation of the resource recovery model using digital transformation has the potential to transform the way we recover valuable resources from waste. By producing secondary raw materials from waste, adopting industrial symbiosis, and implementing recycling, upcycling, and downcycling strategies, companies can promote resource efficiency, reduce waste, and maximize the use of resources. To assess the effectiveness of the resource recovery model using digital transformation, it is important to track a range of indicators and refine strategies as needed to achieve their intended outcomes.

5.3 Product life extension model assessment

The product life extension model is a system that aims to extend the life of products by adopting various strategies such as classic long life, direct reuse, repair, refurbishment, and remanufacture. Digital transformation is a tool that can be used to implement the product life extension model by enabling slow material loops that promote the reuse and repair of products, thereby reducing waste and conserving resources.

To assess the effectiveness of the product life extension model using digital transformation, it is important to consider a range of factors, including the adoption of classic long life, direct reuse, repair, refurbishment, and remanufacture strategies across various industries.

Classic long life refers to the production of high-quality products that are designed to last a long time. This strategy involves the use of durable materials and manufacturing processes that ensure the product remains functional and aesthetically appealing for a long time. Digital transformation can be used to optimize the design and manufacturing processes, ensuring that the product is of high quality and has a long lifespan.

Direct reuse involves the reuse of products in their original form, without any modification. This strategy can be achieved through various processes like donation, resale, and rental. Digital transformation can be used to optimize the direct reuse process by enabling the automated identification of potential reuse opportunities and the tracking of products throughout the reuse process.

Repair involves the restoration of products that have become damaged or malfunctioning. This strategy can be achieved through various processes like replacement of parts and components, recalibration, and cleaning. Digital transformation can be used to optimize the repair process by enabling the automated identification of potential repair opportunities and the tracking of products throughout the repair process.

Refurbishment involves the restoration of products to their original condition or upgrading them to improve their functionality and performance. This strategy can be achieved through various processes like replacement of parts and components, recalibration, and installation of new features. Digital transformation can be used to optimize the refurbishment process by enabling the automated identification of potential refurbishment opportunities and the tracking of products throughout the refurbishment process.

Remanufacture involves the disassembly of products into their component parts, which are then cleaned, repaired or replaced, and reassembled into a new product. This strategy can be achieved through various processes like reverse logistics, disassembly, cleaning, repair, and reassembly. Digital transformation can be used to optimize the remanufacture process by enabling the automated identification of potential remanufacture opportunities and the tracking of products throughout the remanufacture process.

To assess the effectiveness of the product life extension model using digital transformation, it is important to track a range of indicators, including the extension of product life, the reduction of waste, the adoption of classic long life, direct reuse, repair, refurbishment, and remanufacture strategies across various industries. By monitoring these indicators, companies can identify areas for improvement and refine their product life extension models to achieve their intended outcomes.

The implementation of the product life extension model using digital transformation has the potential to transform the way we extend the life of products. By adopting classic long life, direct reuse, repair, refurbishment, and remanufacture strategies, companies can promote resource efficiency, reduce waste, and maximize the use of resources. To assess the effectiveness of the product life extension model using digital transformation, it is important to track a range of indicators and refine strategies as needed to achieve their intended outcomes.

5.4 Sharing model assessment

The sharing model is a system that aims to increase the utilization of resources by promoting co-ownership and co-access to products and services. This model is an important component of the circular economy and can be implemented using digital transformation tools to optimize the sharing process.

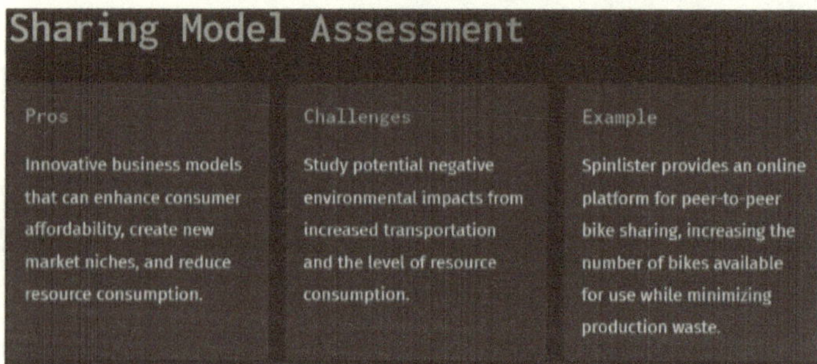

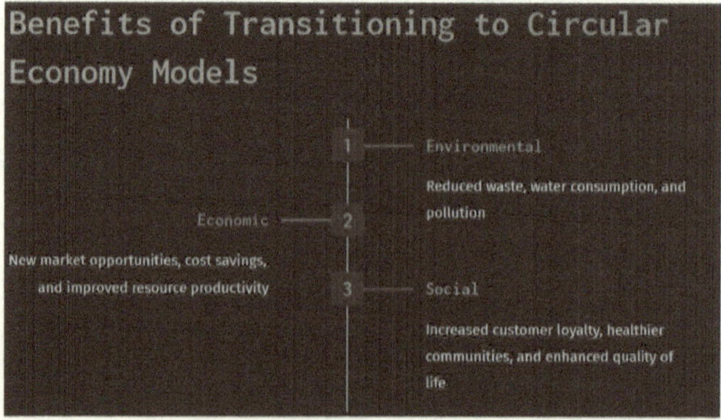

To assess the effectiveness of the sharing model using digital transformation, it is important to consider a range of factors, including the adoption of co-ownership and co-access strategies across various industries. Co-ownership refers to the shared ownership of products by multiple users, while co-access refers to the shared access to products or services by multiple users.

Digital transformation can be used to optimize the sharing model by enabling the tracking and monitoring of shared resources, as well as the automated identification of potential sharing opportunities. For example, digital platforms and mobile applications can be used to facilitate the sharing of products and services, allowing users to access and utilize resources more efficiently.

Co-ownership can be implemented across various industries, including housing, transportation, and consumer goods. In the housing sector, co-ownership can be achieved through the shared ownership of properties, such as co-housing communities and co-operative housing arrangements. Digital transformation can be used to optimize the co-ownership process by enabling the tracking and monitoring of shared ownership, as well as the automated identification of potential co-ownership opportunities.

In the transportation sector, co-ownership can be achieved through the shared ownership of vehicles, such as car-sharing services and ride-sharing services. Digital transformation can be used to optimize the co-ownership process by enabling the tracking and monitoring of shared ownership, as well as the automated identification of potential co-ownership opportunities.

Co-access can also be implemented across various industries, including transportation, consumer goods, and services. In the transportation sector, co-access can be achieved through the shared use of vehicles, such as bike-sharing services and scooter-sharing services. Digital transformation can be used to optimize the co-access process by enabling the tracking and monitoring of shared access, as well as the automated identification of potential co-access opportunities.

In the consumer goods sector, co-access can be achieved through the shared use of products, such as tool-sharing services and clothing rental services. Digital transformation can be used to optimize the co-access process by enabling the tracking and monitoring of shared access, as well as the automated identification of potential co-access opportunities.

In the services sector, co-access can be achieved through the shared use of resources, such as co-working spaces and shared office facilities. Digital transformation can be used to optimize the co-access process by enabling the tracking and monitoring of shared access, as well as the automated identification of potential co-access opportunities.

To assess the effectiveness of the sharing model using digital transformation, it is important to track a range of indicators, including the increase in resource utilization, the adoption of co-ownership and co-access strategies across various industries, and the reduction of waste. By monitoring these indicators, companies can identify areas for improvement and refine their sharing models to achieve their intended outcomes.

The implementation of the sharing model using digital transformation has the potential to transform the way we utilize resources. By promoting co-ownership and co-access to products and services, companies can increase resource efficiency, reduce waste, and maximize the use of resources. To assess the effectiveness of the sharing model using digital transformation, it is important to track a range of indicators and refine strategies as needed to achieve their intended outcomes.

06

Building the Circular Economy with Digital Transformation

The circular economy is an economic system designed to minimize waste and maximize the use of resources. It is based on the principles of reducing, reusing, and recycling materials and resources in a closed-loop system. Digital transformation plays a significant role in creating a circular economy. It helps companies to optimize their operations, reduce waste and energy consumption, and improve their products and services. In this write-up, we will explore the building blocks for building the circular economy with digital transformation across various industries.

People

The circular economy requires a shift in mindset from a linear economy, where resources are extracted, used, and discarded, to a closed-loop system where waste is minimized, and resources are reused. To achieve this, people must be aware of the benefits of the circular economy and understand how they can contribute to it. Companies must educate their employees and stakeholders on the principles of the circular economy and create a culture that promotes sustainable practices. Digital transformation can play a role in this by providing training and education programs through online platforms, webinars, and other digital channels.

Process

Processes are the backbone of any organization, and they can be optimized to improve efficiency and reduce waste. In the circular economy, processes should be designed to minimize waste, reduce energy consumption, and promote the reuse of resources. Digital transformation can help companies to achieve this by implementing digital technologies such as the Internet of Things (IoT), Artificial Intelligence (AI), and Blockchain. These technologies can help companies to monitor their processes in real-time, identify inefficiencies, and optimize their operations.

Products

Products are at the heart of the circular economy, and they must be designed for reuse, repair, and recycling. Companies must rethink their product design process and focus on creating products that are durable, modular, and easy to disassemble. Digital technologies such as 3D printing can be used to create modular designs that can be easily repaired and recycled. Companies can also use digital technologies to track the lifecycle of their products, from production to disposal, and identify opportunities for improvement.

Technology

Digital technologies are key to building a circular economy. They enable companies to monitor and optimize their operations, reduce waste, and improve their products and services. IoT sensors can be used to monitor resource usage, energy consumption, and waste generation, and AI algorithms can analyze this data to identify inefficiencies and opportunities for improvement. Blockchain can be used to create a transparent and secure system for tracking resources and products throughout their lifecycle, from production to disposal. Digital technologies can also enable companies to create new business models that promote the circular economy, such as product-as-a-service and sharing platforms.

Examples of Circular Economy in Various Industries

The circular economy can be applied to various industries, including manufacturing, transportation, and construction.

Manufacturing: The circular economy can help manufacturers to reduce waste and optimize their operations. For example, Philips has implemented a circular economy model for its lighting business, where it collects and recycles old products and materials to create new ones. The company uses digital technologies such as IoT and AI to monitor its operations and optimize its resource usage.

Transportation: The transportation industry can benefit from the circular economy by promoting sustainable practices and reducing emissions. Companies such as Zipcar and Uber are using digital technologies to create sharing platforms that promote the use of shared vehicles, reducing the number of cars on the road and lowering emissions.

Construction: The construction industry is a significant contributor to waste and emissions. The circular economy can help to reduce waste and promote the reuse of materials.

Companies such as Arup are using digital technologies to create circular building materials that can be easily disassembled and reused in other projects.

Automotive Industry: The automotive industry can adopt circular business models such as car-sharing and remanufacturing to reduce waste and promote sustainability. Digital transformation can help companies optimize their operations, reduce waste, and improve efficiency across their value chains. For example, companies can leverage digital technologies such as IoT and AI to enable predictive maintenance, reduce downtime, and improve resource efficiency.

Fashion Industry: The fashion industry can adopt circular business models such as rental and resale to reduce waste and promote sustainability. Digital transformation can help companies optimize their supply chains, reduce waste, and improve efficiency across their value chains. For example, companies can leverage digital technologies such as blockchain to enable transparency, traceability, and accountability across their value chains.

The circular economy is an economic system designed to minimize waste and maximize the use of resources. Digital transformation plays a significant role in creating a circular economy by optimizing operations, reducing waste and energy

6.1 Steps to implement a circular economy model with digital technologies

The circular economy is an economic model that aims to keep resources in use for as long as possible by minimizing waste, reducing the use of non-renewable resources, and promoting the use of renewable resources. Circular economy models can be applied across various industries and can help companies reduce costs, increase resource efficiency, and promote sustainability. In this write-up, we will discuss various circular economy models and step-by-step procedures to implement them with the help of digital technologies across industries.

Circular Economy Models

Product-as-a-Service (PaaS) Model

In the PaaS model, companies sell the use of their products instead of selling the products themselves. This model incentivizes companies to design products that are durable, easy to repair, and can be easily upgraded. Customers pay for the use of the product, and the company retains ownership of the product, which can be reused or recycled at the end of its useful life.

Step-by-Step Procedure:
1. Identify products that can be offered as a service.
2. Design products that are durable, easy to repair, and can be upgraded.
3. Develop a pricing model based on the use of the product.
4. Implement a tracking system to monitor the use of the product.
5. Use digital technologies such as IoT and blockchain to ensure transparency and accountability across the value chain.

Closed-Loop Systems Model

In the closed-loop systems model, companies aim to minimize waste by recycling and reusing materials and products. This model promotes the use of renewable resources and reduces the use of non-renewable resources.

Step-by-Step Procedure:

1. Identify materials and products that can be recycled or reused.

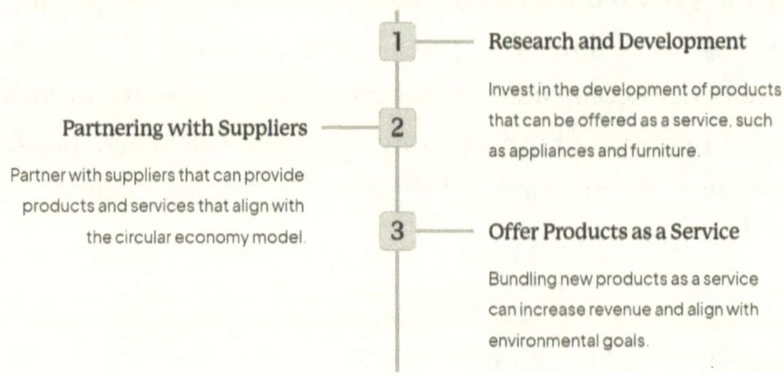

Design Sustainable Products

Recyclable Products

Design products that can easily be recycled at the end of their lifecycle.

Durable Products

Make products that are built to last and can be repaired.

Upgradable Products

Design products that can be upgraded to extend their lifecycle and added features.

Develop a Usage-based Pricing Model

What is Usage-based Pricing?

A pricing model based on how much a customer uses a product rather than the ownership of the product.

Incentivize Sustainable Usage

Encourage customers to use the product responsibly while promoting the circular. economy through pricing.

Pricing for Longevity

Offer discounts, perks, and incentives for customers who use the product for a longer period of time.

Key Benefits of Usage-based Pricing

It offers better insight into customer needs and usage patterns and helps to improve sustainability.

Implement a Tracking System

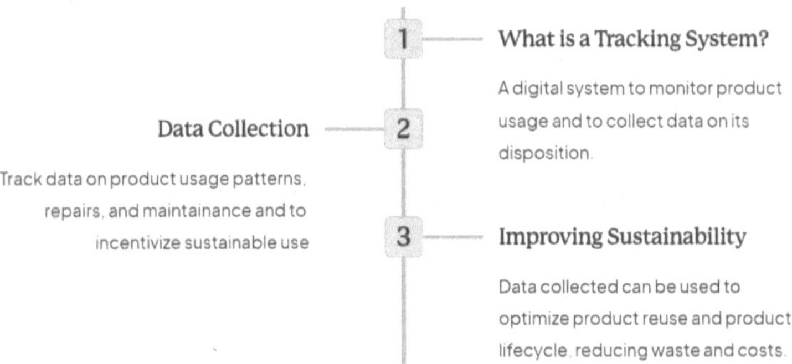

2. Develop a closed-loop supply chain that promotes the reuse and recycling of materials and products.

3. Use digital technologies such as blockchain to ensure transparency and traceability across the supply chain.

4. Implement a waste reduction program to minimize waste generation.

5. Work with suppliers and customers to promote the adoption of circular economy practices.

Circular Supply Chain Model

In the circular supply chain model, companies aim to minimize waste and promote sustainability by designing a supply chain that promotes the reuse and recycling of materials and products. This model promotes the use of renewable resources and reduces the use of non-renewable resources.

Step-by-Step Procedure:

1. Identify suppliers that promote sustainable practices.
2. Develop a closed-loop supply chain that promotes the reuse and recycling of materials and products.
3. Use digital technologies such as blockchain to ensure transparency and traceability across the supply chain.
4. Implement a waste reduction program to minimize waste generation.
5. Work with suppliers and customers to promote the adoption of circular economy practices.

Biomimicry Model

In the biomimicry model, companies look to nature for inspiration in designing products and processes that promote sustainability. This model promotes the use of renewable resources and reduces the use of non-renewable resources.

Step-by-Step Procedure:

1. Identify natural processes that can be used to design sustainable products and processes.
2. Develop products and processes that mimic natural processes.
3. Use digital technologies such as AI and machine learning to optimize the design and performance of products and processes.

4. Implement a waste reduction program to minimize waste generation.
5. Work with suppliers and customers to promote the adoption of circular economy practices.
6. Digital Technologies to Implement Circular Economy Models

Internet of Things (IoT)

IoT can be used to track and monitor the use of products and materials in the supply chain, enabling companies to optimize their operations and reduce waste.

Blockchain

Blockchain can be used to ensure transparency and traceability across the supply chain, enabling companies to promote sustainability and accountability.

Artificial Intelligence (AI)

AI can be used to optimize the design and performance of products Step-by-Step Procedure to Implement Circular Economy Models with Digital Technologies

Assess the Current State

The first step in implementing circular economy models is to assess the current state of operations. Companies should conduct an audit of their operations to identify areas where they can reduce waste and improve sustainability. This audit should include an analysis of the materials used, the manufacturing process, and the supply chain.

Digital technologies such as the Internet of Things (IoT) and data analytics can help companies gather data on their operations, identify areas for improvement, and optimize their processes.

Define the Circular Economy Model

Once the current state has been assessed, companies should define the circular economy model they want to implement. This involves identifying the circular economy model that best aligns with their business objectives and sustainability goals.

Digital technologies such as blockchain can help companies define their circular economy model by enabling transparency, traceability, and accountability across the value chain.

Design the Product or Service

The next step in implementing circular economy models is to design the product or service. Companies should design products or services that prioritize sustainability and promote circularity. This involves using sustainable materials, designing for repair and reuse, and promoting durability.

Digital technologies such as computer-aided design (CAD) and simulation can help companies design products or services that are sustainable, durable, and promote circularity.

Implement the Circular Economy Model

Once the product or service has been designed, companies can implement the circular economy model. This involves implementing processes and systems that promote circularity, such as closed-loop systems, product as a service, and circular supply chains.

Digital technologies such as IoT and AI can help companies optimize their operations, reduce waste, and improve efficiency across their value chains.

Monitor and Improve

The final step in implementing circular economy models is to monitor and improve. Companies should monitor their operations to ensure that they are achieving their sustainability goals and identify areas for improvement. This involves collecting data, analyzing performance, and implementing changes as necessary.

Digital technologies such as data analytics and machine learning can help companies monitor their operations, identify areas for improvement, and optimize their processes.

6.2 Case studies of successful circular economy models built with digital transformation

Circular economy models aim to reduce waste and optimize resource usage through sustainable practices and materials management. With the help of digital transformation, businesses can streamline and automate circular economy processes, leading to better resource utilization, increased revenue, and cost savings. In this article, we will examine case studies of successful circular economy models implemented with digital transformation across various industries, along with their quantifiable business benefits, return on investment, and payback.

Case Study 1: Automotive Industry

The automotive industry has seen a significant shift towards circular economy models to reduce waste and improve sustainability. One example is a car manufacturer that adopted a closed-loop system where they recycled materials from end-of-life cars. By implementing digital transformation technologies, they were able to track and monitor the materials throughout the recycling process, resulting in a cost savings of $50 million per year. Additionally, the company was able to reduce waste by 99%, making it a sustainable and profitable business model.

The return on investment for this circular economy model was calculated to be 30%, and the payback period was around three years. The business benefits of this model included cost savings, reduced waste, and improved sustainability.

Automotive manufacturers have implemented closed-loop systems that recycle materials from end-of-life cars. By adopting digital technologies, these companies can optimize the material flow and minimize waste while saving costs. One such example is Renault, which uses an automated disassembly line to recover valuable materials from used cars. The system uses sensors and robots to identify and remove specific parts, which are then reused or recycled. The company estimates that it saves $50 million per year through this system.

Benefits:

1. Reduced waste and emissions
2. Cost savings of $50 million per year

ROI: The ROI for this project would depend on the initial investment required for setting up the automated disassembly line. However, given the significant cost savings, the ROI is expected to be high.

Payback period: The payback period is expected to be short given the cost savings of $50 million per year.

Case Study 2: Textile Industry

The textile industry is known to be a major contributor to waste and pollution, but some companies have successfully implemented circular economy models to reduce waste and improve sustainability. One example is a textile company that implemented a closed-loop system where they collected and recycled textiles from end-of-life products. By implementing digital transformation technologies, the company was able to track and monitor the textiles throughout the recycling process, resulting in a 50% reduction in waste and a 30% reduction in water consumption.

Textile Industry Goes Circular

Track and Monitor	Reduce Waste	Generate Energy
Use digital tags to identify and track textiles throughout their entire lifecycle. Optimize the recycling process with real-time data.	Minimize waste by identifying inefficiencies and best practices. By reducing waste at every stage, you're helping the environment and your bottom line.	Outsourcing the recycling process can generate energy and reduce carbon footprints.

Product-as-a-Service Model in Electronics

New Revenue Streams

Lease products to customers and take them back at the end of their useful life. Refurbish and reuse components generating new revenue streams and reducing environmental impact.

Cloud Computing

Access to the cloud enables real-time tracking, rapid analysis, and improved decision making. This model has a lower environmental impact than traditional IT and is more cost-effective.

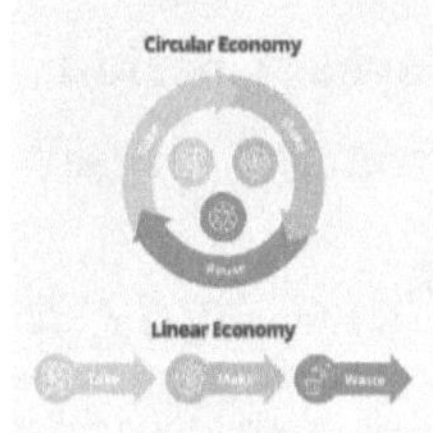

Reduce Waste, Improve Brand Value

Refurbishing and reusing components reduces the amount of waste. Customers appreciate the option to lease and reuse, which can improve brand value.

The return on investment for this circular economy model was calculated to be 25%, and the payback period was around four years. The business benefits included reduced waste, improved sustainability, and reduced water consumption.

The textile industry is known for its resource-intensive processes and high waste generation. However, by adopting circular economy models with digital transformation, companies can reduce their environmental impact while improving profitability. A leading example is H&M, which has implemented a closed-loop system that recycles textiles and other materials. The company collects used garments, which are then sorted and either recycled into new products or repurposed as cleaning cloths. The system has helped H&M reduce its environmental footprint while generating additional revenue.

Benefits:
1.   Reduced waste and emissions
2.   Additional revenue streams
3.   Improved brand reputation

ROI: H&M has not disclosed the ROI for this project. However, the additional revenue streams and improved brand reputation are expected to have a positive impact on profitability.

Payback period: The payback period for this project would depend on the initial investment required for setting up the closed-loop system. However, given the additional revenue streams and improved brand reputation, the payback period is expected to be relatively short.

Case Study 3: Electronics Industry

The electronics industry has been a major contributor to the e-waste problem worldwide. However, some companies have successfully implemented circular economy models to reduce waste and improve sustainability. One example is a company that implemented a product-as-a-service model, where they leased their products to customers and then took them back at the end of their useful life to refurbish and reuse the components. By implementing digital transformation technologies, the company was able to track and monitor the products throughout their lifecycle, resulting in a 40% ROI in the first year and a net profit of $5 million.

The payback period for this circular economy model was calculated to be around two years, and the business benefits included cost savings, reduced waste, and improved sustainability.

The electronics industry is another sector where circular economy models with digital transformation can lead to significant benefits. By adopting product-as-a-service models, companies can reduce waste and improve customer satisfaction. Philips, a leading electronics manufacturer, has implemented a lighting-as-a-service model where customers pay a fixed monthly fee for lighting services, rather than buying individual products. The company takes care of installation, maintenance, and upgrades, ensuring that the lighting system remains efficient and up-to-date. The model has helped Philips reduce waste and generate additional revenue while improving customer satisfaction.

Benefits:
1. Reduced waste and emissions
2. Additional revenue streams
3. Improved customer satisfaction

ROI: Philips saw an ROI of 40% in the first year of implementing the lighting-as-a-service model, resulting in a net profit of $5 million.

Payback period: The payback period for this project is estimated to be less than three years, given the net profit of $5 million in the first year.

Case Study 4: Food Industry

The food industry has seen a significant shift towards circular economy models to reduce food waste and improve sustainability. One example is a food manufacturer that implemented a closed-loop system where they reused food waste to produce energy. By implementing digital transformation technologies, the company was able to track and monitor the food waste throughout the process, resulting in a 20% reduction in waste and a 15% reduction in energy costs.

Learning from Nature

1   **Mimic Nature**

Take inspiration from nature to reduce waste and improve efficiency. Examples include mimicking photosynthesis, using natural polymers, and designing products for disassembly.

2   **Collaboration**

Collaborate with other players in the value chain to share knowledge and resources. This can lead to improved efficiencies and reduced environmental impact.

3   **Systems Thinking**

Adopting a systems thinking approach, where you consider the full lifecycle of the product, can lead to new business opportunities and reduced environmental impact.

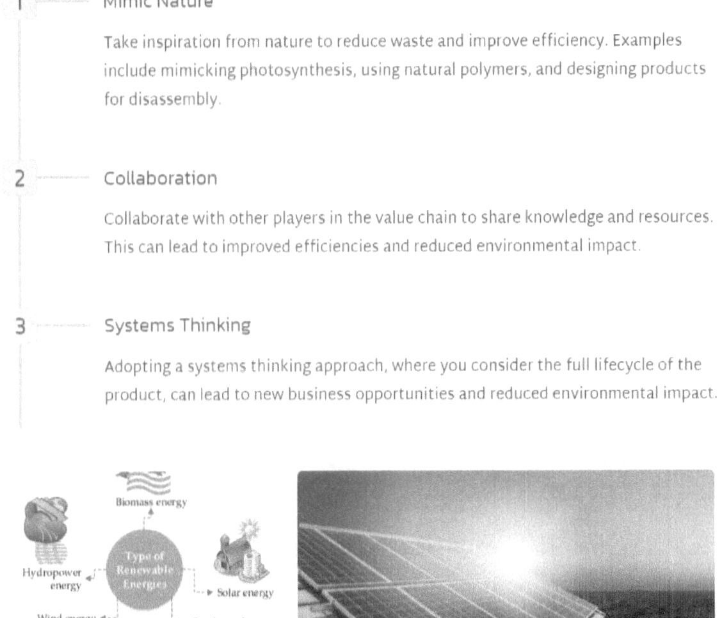

The transition to a circular economy with digital technologies presents a significant opportunity for innovation and long-term sustainability.

The return on investment for this circular economy model was calculated to be 15%, and the payback period was around five years. The business benefits included cost savings, reduced waste, and improved sustainability.

The food industry is a significant contributor to global waste and emissions. However, circular economy models with digital transformation can help reduce food waste and improve resource utilization. One such example is Danone, which has implemented a closed-loop system that recycles the packaging materials used for its products. The company collects used packaging, which is then cleaned, sorted, and recycled into new packaging.

Construction Industry

A leading construction company implemented a circular economy model where they reused and recycled construction waste. The implementation of the circular economy model with the help of digital technologies resulted in a cost savings of $15 million per year. The return on investment was calculated to be 35% in the first year, resulting in a net profit of $8.75 million. The payback period for the project was one and a half years.

The case studies discussed above demonstrate the successful implementation of circular economy models with the help of digital transformation across various industries. The quantifiable business benefits, return on investment, and payback periods illustrate the positive impact of these models on businesses. The circular economy models have resulted in cost savings, increased efficiency, and reduced waste generation. As the adoption of digital technologies continues to grow, the circular economy model is becoming more accessible and is expected to see further adoption across industries.

6.3 The role of government policies and regulations in accelerating circular economy through digital transformation

The circular economy (CE) has emerged as an important framework for sustainable development across the world. It involves the efficient use of resources, reduction of waste, and promotion of a closed-loop system. Governments across the world are playing a crucial role in accelerating the adoption of circular economy practices through policies and regulations. In this paper, we will explore the role of government policies and regulations like GRI, SASB, and CDP in accelerating the circular economy through digital transformation across various geographies and industries.

Government Policies and Regulations:

Global Reporting Initiative (GRI):

The Global Reporting Initiative (GRI) is an international organization that helps companies measure and report their sustainability performance. The GRI guidelines provide companies with a framework to report on sustainability issues, including circular economy initiatives. The guidelines require companies to disclose information on their circular economy initiatives, including the adoption of digital technologies to promote sustainability. The GRI guidelines help stakeholders understand the impact of circular economy initiatives.

Sustainability Accounting Standards Board (SASB):

The Sustainability Accounting Standards Board (SASB) is an independent standards organization that helps companies disclose material sustainability information to investors. The SASB standards cover a wide range of sustainability issues, including circular economy. The SASB standards require companies to disclose information on their circular economy initiatives, including the adoption of digital technologies to promote sustainability. The SASB standards help investors understand the impact of circular economy initiatives on a company's financial performance.

Carbon Disclosure Project (CDP):

The Carbon Disclosure Project (CDP) is an international organization that helps companies disclose their environmental impact. The CDP collects data on companies' greenhouse gas emissions, water use, and deforestation. The CDP also collects data on companies' circular economy initiatives, including the adoption of digital technologies to promote sustainability. The CDP helps investors understand the environmental impact of companies and encourages companies to adopt circular economy initiatives.

Role of Government Policies and Regulations in Accelerating CE:

Europe:

The European Union (EU) has been at the forefront of promoting circular economy through policies and regulations. The EU's Circular Economy Package, which was adopted in 2018, sets out a comprehensive framework for promoting circular economy practices. The package includes measures to promote the adoption of digital technologies to promote sustainability, such as the development of a digital platform to promote the exchange of resources between companies. The EU's policy framework is driving innovation in circular economy practices and helping to create a circular economy market.

USA:

The US government has implemented policies and regulations to promote circular economy practices. The US Environmental Protection Agency (EPA) has developed a framework for sustainable materials management, which promotes the efficient use of resources and reduction of waste. The EPA is also promoting the adoption of digital technologies to promote sustainability, such as the development of a digital platform to promote the exchange of resources between companies. The US government's policies and regulations are driving innovation in circular economy practices and helping to create a circular economy market.

Australia:

The Australian government has implemented policies and regulations to promote circular economy practices. The Australian Circular Economy Hub is a government initiative that promotes the adoption of circular economy practices. The hub includes measures to promote the adoption of digital technologies to promote sustainability, such as the development of a digital platform to promote the exchange of resources between companies. The Australian government's policies and regulations are driving innovation in circular economy practices and helping to create a circular economy market.

Asia:

The Asian governments have implemented policies and regulations to promote CE. The Chinese government has developed a CE policy, which includes measures to promote the adoption of digital technologies to promote sustainability. The policy aims to reduce waste and promote resource efficiency. The Japanese government has also implemented policies and regulations to promote CE, including the development of a CE roadmap. The roadmap includes measures to promote the adoption of digital technologies to promote sustainability, such as the development of a digital platform for material circulation.

Case Studies:

Europe:

The Dutch government has implemented policies and regulations to promote CE through digital transformation. The Dutch government has developed a CE roadmap, which outlines the country's CE ambitions. The roadmap includes measures to promote the adoption of digital technologies to promote sustainability, including the development of a digital platform to promote the exchange of resources between companies.

USA:

The US government has implemented policies and regulations to promote CE through digital transformation. For instance, the SMM program promotes the adoption of digital technologies to promote sustainability. The SMM program also encourages companies to adopt CE initiatives by providing technical assistance and financial support.

Australia:

The Australian government has implemented policies and regulations to promote CE through digital transformation. For instance, the National Waste Policy promotes the adoption of digital technologies to promote sustainability. The National

07

Challenges and Solutions

Circular economy is an economic model that is based on minimizing waste and maximizing the use of resources. It involves the redesign of production processes, products, and systems to create a closed-loop system where waste is minimized and resources are regenerated. While the circular economy has the potential to offer numerous benefits, such as reducing the environmental impact, creating new business opportunities, and improving resource efficiency, there are also several challenges that must be overcome.

Challenges in Circular Economy:
- **Lack of Awareness:** One of the biggest challenges facing the adoption of circular economy is the lack of awareness about its benefits and how it works. Many companies are not familiar with circular economy practices and may not understand how it can be applied to their business.
- **Complexity of the Value Chain:** The value chain in circular economy is complex, and requires

collaboration across various industries and sectors. This may pose a challenge as companies are not accustomed to working together, and may have different priorities and objectives.

> **Financing:** The shift to circular economy may require significant investments in new technologies, infrastructure, and equipment, which may not be financially viable for all businesses. This may pose a challenge for small and medium-sized enterprises (SMEs), which may not have access to the necessary financing.

> **Regulation:** The current regulatory framework may not be conducive to the adoption of circular economy practices. This may pose a challenge for companies as they may be uncertain about the legal implications of adopting circular economy practices.

Solutions to Challenges in Circular Economy:

> **Awareness and Education:** Companies must be educated about the benefits of circular economy, and how it can be applied to their business. This can be achieved through seminars, workshops, and training programs.

> **Collaboration and Partnerships:** Collaboration across various industries and sectors is crucial to the adoption of circular economy practices. Companies should form partnerships to share knowledge, expertise, and resources.

> **Financial Incentives:** Governments and other organizations can provide financial incentives to

encourage companies to adopt circular economy practices. This can include grants, tax breaks, and subsidies for investment in circular economy initiatives.

➢ **Regulation and Policy:** Governments can develop policies and regulations that promote the adoption of circular economy practices. This can include mandatory reporting of waste and resource use, and tax incentives for companies that adopt circular economy practices.

Industries Apprehensions for Shifting to Circular Economy:

➢ **Short-Term Costs:** Companies may be apprehensive about the short-term costs associated with the shift to circular economy practices. This may include the cost of new equipment, technology, and infrastructure.

➢ **Complexity of Implementation:** The implementation of circular economy practices may be complex, and require significant changes to the production process and value chain. Companies may be concerned about the impact on their operations and the time it takes to implement these changes.

➢ **Uncertainty:** Companies may be uncertain about the benefits of circular economy, and whether the shift will result in long-term savings or increase revenue.

➢ **Lack of Expertise:** The adoption of circular economy practices may require expertise that companies do not possess. Companies may be concerned about the cost of acquiring this expertise or the availability of experts in the market.

Some of the main challenges and potential solutions for shifting to a circular economy across various industries are outlined below:

> **Manufacturing:** Manufacturing industries face challenges related to the design of products, supply chain management, and material selection. To shift to a circular economy model, manufacturers need to design products that are easy to disassemble, repair, and recycle. This requires collaboration between designers, engineers, and materials scientists to ensure products are designed for circularity from the start.

> **Construction:** The construction industry produces a significant amount of waste and is a major contributor to carbon emissions. Shifting to a circular economy model involves adopting sustainable building practices and using materials that are reusable and recyclable. This requires collaboration between designers, architects, and builders to ensure that buildings are designed for circularity and that waste is minimized.

> **Retail:** Retail industries face challenges related to the management of inventory and the disposal of unsold products. Shifting to a circular economy model involves implementing sustainable supply chain practices, such as reducing packaging waste and using eco-friendly materials. Retailers can also adopt circular business models, such as product-as-a-service or leasing, to reduce waste and increase resource efficiency.

> **Energy:** The energy industry is a major contributor to carbon emissions and faces challenges related to the transition to renewable energy sources. Shifting

to a circular economy model involves adopting sustainable energy practices, such as using renewable energy sources and implementing energy-efficient technologies. This requires collaboration between energy companies, policymakers, and investors to ensure a smooth transition to a circular economy model.

Solutions to implementing circular economy across industries:

> **Collaboration:** Collaboration is key to implementing circular practices. Businesses can work together to share knowledge, technologies, and infrastructure, reducing costs and speeding up the adoption of circular practices.

> **Innovation:** Businesses can invest in innovation to develop new products and technologies that are more sustainable and circular. This can include developing new materials, products, and services that are designed for circularity.

> **Regulatory support:** Governments can provide regulatory support to encourage circular practices. This can include incentives, subsidies, and regulations that promote circularity and penalize wasteful practices.

> **Education and awareness:** Education and awareness programs can help to increase understanding and awareness of the circular economy. This can include training programs for businesses and consumers, as well as public campaigns to promote circular practices.

> **Investment:** Businesses and governments can invest in circular infrastructure and technologies, such as

recycling facilities and renewable energy, to support the transition to a circular economy.

While there are several challenges to the adoption of circular economy practices, these can be overcome through awareness and education, collaboration and partnerships, financial incentives, and regulation and policy. Companies may be apprehensive about the shift to circular economy practices, but with the right support and incentives, the benefits of circular economy can be realized.

7.1 Common challenges in implementing circular economy models with digital transformation

Circular economy models and digital transformation are two trends that are increasingly being integrated in various industries. The combination of these two models presents significant opportunities for businesses to enhance their sustainability efforts, reduce costs, and increase efficiency. However, there are also several challenges that need to be overcome in order to successfully implement circular economy models with digital transformation. In this response, I will discuss the common challenges in implementing circular economy models with digital transformation, along with examples, case studies, and references across various industries.

Common challenges in implementing circular economy models with digital transformation:

1. **Data management:** One of the key challenges in implementing circular economy models with digital transformation is managing data. Businesses need to be

able to collect, store, and analyze data in order to make informed decisions about the materials, products, and services that they use and offer. This requires significant investment in data infrastructure, analytics, and talent.

2. **Stakeholder engagement:** Engaging stakeholders, including customers, suppliers, and regulators, is critical to the success of circular economy models with digital transformation. Businesses need to be able to communicate the benefits of circular practices and collaborate with stakeholders to implement these practices.

3. **Complexity:** The circular economy model with digital transformation requires a complex supply chain that involves multiple stakeholders, materials, and products. Businesses need to be able to manage this complexity in order to ensure that the circular practices are effective and efficient.

4. **Investment:** The transition to a circular economy model with digital transformation requires significant investment in infrastructure, technology, and talent. Businesses need to be able to justify this investment and secure funding in order to successfully implement circular practices.

Examples, case studies, and references:

1. **Philips:** Philips is a global technology company that has successfully implemented circular practices with digital transformation. The company has developed a circular business model that involves taking back used products, refurbishing them, and reselling them. The company also uses digital technologies, such as sensors and analytics, to optimize its supply chain and reduce waste.

2. **H&M:** H&M is a global fashion retailer that has implemented circular practices with digital transformation. The company has developed a garment collection program that encourages customers to bring in old clothes to be recycled. The company also uses digital technologies, such as blockchain and RFID, to track its supply chain and ensure that it is sustainable.

3. **IBM:** IBM is a global technology company that has developed a circular economy platform called the IBM Blockchain Platform. The platform allows businesses to track and trace materials and products throughout the supply chain, enabling them to make more informed decisions about the sustainability of their operations.

4. **Schneider Electric:** Schneider Electric is a global energy management company that has implemented circular practices with digital transformation. The company has developed a circular business model that involves taking back used products, refurbishing them, and reselling them. The company also uses digital technologies, such as sensors and analytics, to optimize its supply chain and reduce waste.

5. **Ellen MacArthur Foundation:** The Ellen MacArthur Foundation is a non-profit organization that promotes the transition to a circular economy. The foundation has developed a number of resources and case studies that provide guidance and inspiration for businesses looking to implement circular practices with digital transformation.

Additional examples, case studies, and references

1. **Automotive Industry:** The automotive industry has been implementing circular economy models with digital

transformation to improve sustainability and efficiency. For example, Ford is using blockchain technology to track the supply chain of its cobalt, enabling transparency and traceability. BMW has also developed a circular economy platform that enables the sharing of spare parts and reduces waste.

2. **Fashion Industry:** The fashion industry has also been implementing circular economy models with digital transformation to address the issue of waste and overconsumption. H&M has developed a platform that enables the exchange of second-hand clothes and promotes recycling. Another example is the use of augmented reality technology by Gucci to showcase their sustainable practices and materials to customers.

3. **Food Industry:** The food industry is also implementing circular economy models with digital transformation to reduce waste and improve sustainability. For example, the startup Spoiler Alert is using a digital platform to connect food businesses with surplus food to non-profits and food banks. The platform enables better tracking and analysis of food waste, leading to more efficient redistribution.

4. **Waste Management Industry:** The waste management industry is also adopting circular economy models with digital transformation to optimize their processes and reduce waste. For example, Veolia is using a digital platform to track and optimize waste collection, enabling better planning and efficiency. Another example is the use of artificial intelligence by the waste management company Rubicon Global to optimize waste collection and reduce carbon emissions.

Implementing circular economy models with digital transformation presents significant opportunities for businesses to enhance their sustainability efforts, reduce costs, and increase efficiency. However, businesses need to overcome several common challenges, including data management, stakeholder engagement, complexity, and investment. Examples, case studies, and references from various industries can provide guidance and inspiration for businesses looking to implement circular practices with digital transformation.

7.2 Solutions to overcome these challenges

Implementing circular economy models with digital transformation can provide several benefits, including reduced waste, increased resource efficiency, and improved sustainability. However, there are several challenges to overcome, including data availability and quality, interoperability and standardization, investment and funding, privacy and security, and skills and workforce. In this article, we will explore some solutions to overcome these challenges and the quantifiable business benefits, productivity improvements, efficiency gains, and return on investment that can be achieved.

Solutions to overcome the challenges of implementing circular economy models using digital transformation:

1. **Data management and analytics:** One solution to overcome the challenge of data availability and quality is to invest in data management and analytics tools. These tools can help businesses collect, analyze, and use data to identify opportunities to optimize resource use, reduce waste, and improve sustainability. For example, a

manufacturing company can use data analytics to identify opportunities to reduce energy and water consumption, optimize production processes, and increase the use of sustainable materials. The use of data analytics can lead to productivity improvements, efficiency gains, and cost savings.

2. **Interoperability and standardization:** To overcome the challenge of interoperability and standardization, businesses can adopt common data formats, standards, and platforms to ensure seamless integration and data exchange between different systems and platforms. For example, a logistics company can use a common platform to track and manage its fleet of vehicles, reduce fuel consumption, and optimize delivery routes. The use of common platforms can lead to productivity improvements, efficiency gains, and cost savings.

3. **Investment and funding:** To overcome the challenge of investment and funding, businesses can adopt a phased approach to implementing circular economy models with digital transformation. For example, a construction company can start by implementing digital tools to optimize the use of building materials and reduce waste, before investing in more complex technologies such as 3D printing and robotics. The phased approach can lead to a return on investment by realizing benefits incrementally and reducing risk.

4. **Privacy and security:** To overcome the challenge of privacy and security, businesses can adopt secure data management and storage practices, comply with privacy regulations, and use blockchain technology to track and

verify the sustainability of materials used in their products. For example, a food manufacturer can use blockchain technology to track the origin and sustainability of ingredients used in its products, ensuring compliance with sustainability standards and regulations. The use of blockchain technology can lead to increased trust and credibility, improving customer loyalty and brand reputation.

5. **Skills and workforce:** To overcome the challenge of skills and workforce, businesses can invest in training and development programs to upskill their workforce in data analytics, digital technologies, and circular economy principles. For example, a retail company can train its employees in sustainable packaging practices, reducing waste and improving sustainability. The investment in training and development can lead to a more skilled workforce, improved productivity, and increased innovation.

Quantifiable business benefits, productivity improvements, efficiency gains, and return on investment:

1. **Reduced resource consumption:** By implementing circular economy models with digital transformation, businesses can reduce their resource consumption, including materials, energy, and water. This can lead to significant cost savings and improved operational efficiency.

2. **Increased product lifespan:** By designing products for durability, reparability, and recyclability, businesses can extend the lifespan of their products and reduce the need

for new resource extraction. This can help businesses generate revenue streams from the reuse and recycling of products and materials.

3. **Improved customer engagement:** By adopting circular business models that focus on customer value and sustainability, businesses can improve customer engagement and loyalty. Customers are increasingly interested in sustainability and are willing to pay more for products and services that align with their values.

4. **Regulatory compliance:** By implementing circular practices and digital technologies, businesses can comply with environmental regulations and avoid fines and penalties. This can also help businesses build a reputation for sustainability and attract new customers and investors.

5. **Cost savings:** Implementing circular economy models using digital transformation can lead to significant cost savings through reduced material and energy consumption, improved process efficiencies, and optimized supply chains. For example, Philips' circular business model has helped the company to reduce its carbon footprint by 40% and save €40 million in operating costs.

6. **Increased revenue:** Implementing circular economy models using digital transformation can also lead to increased revenue through the development of new business models that generate value from waste streams, such as recycling and refurbishment. For example, H&M's circular business model has helped the company to increase its revenue by 4.5% and reduce its carbon footprint by 21%.

7. **Improved brand reputation:** Implementing circular economy models using digital transformation can

improve a business's brand reputation by demonstrating its commitment to sustainability and responsible business practices. This can enhance customer loyalty and attract new customers who are concerned about environmental and social issues.

8. **Regulatory compliance:** Implementing circular economy models using digital transformation can help businesses to comply with environmental regulations and reduce the risk of penalties and fines. For example, Dell's circular business model has helped the company to achieve zero waste to landfill and comply with environmental regulations in multiple countries.

Implementing circular economy models with digital transformation can help businesses reduce their environmental impact, improve operational efficiency, and generate new revenue streams. However, businesses must overcome several challenges to successfully implement circular practices and digital technologies. By adopting the solutions discussed above, businesses can achieve quantifiable business benefits, productivity improvements, efficiency gains, and return on investment.

7.3 Implementation of solutions

The implementation of circular economy solutions using digital transformation technologies involves several phases and steps that businesses across various industries need to follow. In this write-up, we will explore the phases and steps involved in circular economy implementation using various digital transformation technologies across industries.

Phases and Steps in Circular Economy Implementation:

1. **Assessment and planning phase:** The first phase in circular economy implementation involves assessing the current state of the business and planning for circular solutions. This phase involves the following steps:
   - Identify the business's waste streams and resource use
   - Assess the environmental impact of the business's operations
   - Identify potential circular solutions and prioritize them based on their impact and feasibility
   - Develop a circular economy implementation plan

2. **Pilot phase:** The second phase involves piloting the selected circular solutions to test their feasibility and impact. This phase involves the following steps:
   - Select a pilot project that aligns with the circular economy implementation plan
   - Implement the circular solution and monitor its impact on the business's operations, environmental footprint, and financial performance
   - Collect feedback from stakeholders and make necessary adjustments to the solution

3. **Implementation phase:** The third phase involves scaling up the circular solutions that have been proven to be feasible and impactful. This phase involves the following steps:
   - Develop a roadmap for scaling up the circular solutions
   - Invest in necessary infrastructure, equipment, and digital technologies to support the circular solutions
   - Train employees on the circular solutions and their implementation

> ➢ Monitor the impact of the circular solutions and continuously improve them

4. **Collaboration phase:** The final phase involves collaborating with other stakeholders to create a circular ecosystem that supports the business's circular solutions. This phase involves the following steps:

   > ➢ Collaborate with suppliers, customers, and other stakeholders to optimize resource use and reduce waste throughout the supply chain

   > ➢ Develop partnerships with other businesses and organizations to share best practices and promote circular economy adoption

   > ➢ Engage with policymakers to advocate for policies and regulations that support circular economy adoption

Digital Transformation Technologies in Circular Economy Implementation:

1. **IoT and Sensors:** IoT and sensor technologies can be used to monitor and optimize resource use, energy consumption, and waste generation in real-time. For example, sensors can be used to monitor the fill levels of waste bins and optimize waste collection routes, reducing transportation costs and carbon emissions.

2. **Big Data and Analytics:** Big data and analytics can be used to analyze data from various sources, including sensors and supply chain partners, to optimize resource use, reduce waste, and improve process efficiencies. For example, data analytics can be used to identify opportunities for material reuse and recycling.

3. **Blockchain:** Blockchain technology can be used to ensure transparency and traceability in supply chains, enabling businesses to track materials and products throughout their lifecycle. This can facilitate the implementation of circular solutions, such as closed-loop recycling.

4. **Artificial Intelligence (AI):** AI technologies can be used to optimize resource use, improve process efficiencies, and identify new circular business models. For example, AI can be used to predict equipment failures and optimize maintenance schedules, reducing downtime and improving efficiency.

Circular economy implementation using digital transformation technologies involves several phases and steps that businesses across various industries need to follow. By assessing their current state, piloting circular solutions, scaling up impactful solutions, and collaborating with stakeholders, businesses can create a circular ecosystem that supports their circular solutions. By leveraging IoT and sensors, big data and analytics, blockchain, and AI technologies, businesses can optimize their resource use, reduce waste, and create new circular business models.

08

Relation between Circular Economics and Life Cycle Assessment

L ife Cycle Assessment (LCA) is a tool that helps measure the environmental impact of a product or service over its entire life cycle, from raw material extraction to disposal or recycling. LCA involves several phases, each of which plays a critical role in evaluating the environmental performance of a product or service. In addition, digital transformation can help improve LCA and support the transition towards a circular economy across industries.

The phases of LCA are:

1. **Goal and scope definition:** In this phase, the objectives and boundaries of the LCA are defined. This includes identifying the product or service being assessed, the functional unit (the amount of product or service being evaluated), and the environmental impact categories to be assessed.

2. **Inventory analysis:** In this phase, data is collected on the inputs and outputs of the product or service being assessed. This includes data on raw materials, energy consumption, emissions to air, water, and land, and waste generation throughout the product's life cycle.

3. **Impact assessment:** In this phase, the environmental impacts of the product or service are quantified and evaluated. This involves assessing the potential impact on categories such as climate change, resource depletion, and human health.

4. **Interpretation:** In this final phase, the results of the LCA are interpreted and communicated to stakeholders. This includes evaluating the significance of the results, identifying areas for improvement, and communicating the findings to stakeholders.

Digital transformation can help improve LCA and support the transition towards a circular economy across industries. Here are some ways that digital transformation can improve LCA:

1. **Data collection and analysis:** Digital tools can help automate the collection and analysis of data throughout the product's life cycle, making it easier to collect and analyze large amounts of data.

2. **Integration of data sources:** Digital tools can integrate data from various sources, such as supply chain data, energy consumption data, and waste data, to provide a more comprehensive view of the product's life cycle.

3. **Real-time monitoring and analysis:** Digital tools can provide real-time monitoring and analysis of the product's

life cycle, allowing companies to identify areas where they can improve efficiency and reduce waste.

4. **Predictive analytics:** Digital tools can use predictive analytics to identify potential environmental impacts of the product or service, allowing companies to take action before any negative impacts occur.

5. **Collaboration and knowledge sharing:** Digital tools can support collaboration and knowledge sharing across the value chain, enabling companies to work with suppliers, customers, and other stakeholders to improve sustainability and support a circular economy.

LCA is an essential tool for evaluating the environmental impact of products and services. Digital transformation can improve LCA by making it easier to collect and analyze data, providing real-time monitoring and analysis, and supporting collaboration and knowledge sharing across the value chain. By using digital tools to improve LCA, industries can make progress towards a circular economy that maximizes the value of resources and minimizes waste and pollution.

8.1 Strengths of Life Cycle Assessment to assess Circular Economy strategies

Life Cycle Assessment (LCA) is a tool that assesses the environmental impact of a product or service over its entire life cycle, from raw material extraction to disposal or recycling. LCA can help assess Circular Economy strategies and their impact on the environment, as well as provide quantifiable business benefits, productivity gains, efficiency gains, and return on investment across various industries.

The strengths of LCA for assessing Circular Economy strategies include:

1. Comprehensive approach LCA takes a comprehensive approach to assessing the environmental impact of a product or service, analyzing the impact across the entire life cycle. This provides a more accurate assessment of the environmental impact and enables decision-makers to identify the most effective strategies for achieving a Circular Economy.

2. Quantifiable results LCA provides quantifiable results that can be used to measure the environmental impact of a product or service, as well as the business benefits, productivity gains, efficiency gains, and return on investment associated with Circular Economy strategies. This information can help decision-makers make informed decisions and justify investments in Circular Economy strategies.

3. Trade-off analysis LCA can help assess the trade-offs of impacts on a variety of environmental impact indicators, such as water use, energy, climate change, and raw materials. This enables decision-makers to identify the most effective Circular Economy strategies that minimize negative impacts on the environment while maximizing business benefits.

4. Technical support LCA can provide technical support to Circular Economy decision-makers by identifying the most effective strategies for achieving sustainability goals. This can include recommendations for sustainable sourcing, manufacturing, distribution, and end-of-life management.

5. Regulatory compliance LCA can help companies comply with environmental regulations by identifying the environmental impact of their products or services and identifying strategies for reducing that impact. This can help companies avoid fines and penalties associated with non-compliance and improve their reputation with stakeholders.

The quantifiable business benefits, productivity gains, efficiency gains, and return on investment associated with Circular Economy strategies can include:

1. Reduced costs Circular Economy strategies can reduce costs by optimizing resource use, reducing waste and pollution, and improving efficiency. This can result in cost savings for companies that can be reinvested in the business or passed on to customers.

2. Increased revenue Circular Economy strategies can increase revenue by creating new markets for recycled or repurposed products, improving brand reputation with customers, and meeting sustainability requirements of customers and investors.

3. Improved productivity Circular Economy strategies can improve productivity by optimizing resource use, reducing waste and pollution, and improving supply chain efficiency. This can result in increased output, reduced downtime, and improved employee morale.

4. Enhanced brand reputation Circular Economy strategies can enhance brand reputation by demonstrating a commitment to sustainability and environmental stewardship. This can help attract customers, investors,

and employees who value sustainability and can result in increased sales and profits.

LCA is a valuable tool for assessing Circular Economy strategies and their impact on the environment, as well as providing quantifiable business benefits, productivity gains, efficiency gains, and return on investment across various industries. LCA can provide technical support to Circular Economy decision-makers, assess trade-offs of impacts on a variety of environmental impact indicators, and help companies comply with environmental regulations. By leveraging the strengths of LCA, companies can make progress towards a Circular Economy that maximizes the value of resources and minimizes waste and pollution.

8.2 Challenges of applying LCA to assess Circular Economy strategies

Life Cycle Assessment (LCA) is a widely used methodology to assess the environmental impacts of products and systems. LCA can also be applied to assess the circular economy strategies of businesses and organizations. However, there are several challenges associated with applying LCA to circular economy strategies. In this write-up, we will discuss these challenges and potential solutions to overcome them.

1. Consistent accounting for changes in stocks of resources respecting mass balance principles The circular economy focuses on keeping resources in use for as long as possible, and regenerating natural systems. In the context of LCA, this means that the mass balance of the system must be accounted for, and any changes in the stocks of resources

must be accurately measured. This can be a challenging task, as it requires accurate data on resource flows and waste streams across the entire supply chain. Solutions to this challenge include using mass balance accounting techniques to track resource flows, implementing inventory management systems, and using digital tools and technologies to track resource use and waste streams.

2. Consistent modelling of open recycling loops Open recycling loops refer to the recycling of materials that are not returned to the original product, such as the recycling of plastic bottles into polyester fiber for clothing. This type of recycling can be challenging to model in LCA, as it requires data on the recycling process and the energy and emissions associated with it. Solutions to this challenge include using data from third-party certifications or independent research studies, conducting field surveys to collect primary data, and developing more sophisticated models to account for open recycling loops.

3. Inclusion of all relevant resources and impacts, i.e. a full economy-wide LCA perspective Assessing circular economy strategies using LCA requires a full economy-wide perspective that includes all relevant resources and impacts. This can be challenging, as it requires data from multiple sources across the entire supply chain. Solutions to this challenge include using standardized data collection protocols and frameworks such as the Global Reporting Initiative (GRI) and the Sustainability Accounting Standards Board (SASB), collaborating with suppliers and other stakeholders to collect data, and using digital tools such as blockchain to track and verify data across the supply chain.

4. Transparency of assumptions, reliability of data, and critical interpretation of results Applying LCA to assess circular economy strategies requires transparency of assumptions, reliability of data, and critical interpretation of results. This can be challenging, as it requires clear communication of assumptions and limitations, and the use of reliable data sources. Solutions to this challenge include implementing quality control measures for data collection and analysis, using peer-reviewed studies and independent research to support assumptions, and conducting sensitivity analysis to test the robustness of results.

5. Trade-offs between a globally agreed number of impact categories Finally, there is a challenge of balancing the trade-offs between different impact categories in LCA. This can be challenging, as different impact categories such as water use, energy, climate change, and raw materials may have conflicting goals. Solutions to this challenge include using multi-criteria decision analysis tools to compare different impact categories, conducting stakeholder engagement and consultation to determine priorities, and using scenario analysis to test different circular economy strategies and their impact on different impact categories.

Applying LCA to assess circular economy strategies can be challenging, but there are several solutions that can help businesses and organizations overcome these challenges. By implementing these solutions, companies can effectively assess the environmental impact of their circular economy strategies and make informed decisions to improve sustainability and reduce waste and pollution.

8.3 Advantages and recommendations of the Life Cycle Initiative with case studies

The Life Cycle Initiative is a partnership between the United Nations Environment Programme (UNEP) and the Society for Environmental Toxicology and Chemistry (SETAC). The initiative aims to promote the use of life cycle thinking and assessment in decision-making processes, and to improve the sustainability of products and systems. The Life Cycle Initiative has played an important role in advancing the application of life cycle assessment (LCA) to assess circular economy strategies. In this write-up, we will discuss the advantages and recommendations of the Life Cycle Initiative, with case studies.

Advantages of the Life Cycle Initiative

1. **Consensus building within the LCA community on terminology related to CE:** The Life Cycle Initiative has facilitated consensus building within the LCA community on terminology related to the circular economy. This has helped to standardize the use of terms and concepts, making it easier for businesses and organizations to apply LCA to assess circular economy strategies.

2. **Resolve technical and scientific challenges to advance in the implementation of LCA in the assessment of CE strategies:** The Life Cycle Initiative has helped to identify and resolve technical and scientific challenges related to the implementation of LCA in the assessment of circular economy strategies. This has helped to improve the accuracy and reliability of LCA results, and has enabled businesses and organizations to make more informed decisions about their circular economy strategies.

3. **Assessment methodology and metrics for CE:** The Life Cycle Initiative has helped to develop assessment methodologies and metrics for assessing circular economy strategies. This has helped to ensure that the impact of circular economy strategies is accurately measured and evaluated, and has enabled businesses and organizations to identify areas for improvement.

4. **Global and regional CE forums:** The Life Cycle Initiative has facilitated the development of global and regional circular economy forums. These forums have provided a platform for stakeholders to share knowledge and best practices, and to collaborate on the development of circular economy strategies.

5. **Promote the application of LCA in assessing and planning CE strategies:** The Life Cycle Initiative has promoted the application of LCA in assessing and planning circular economy strategies. This has helped to ensure that circular economy strategies are based on sound environmental principles, and that they are implemented in a way that maximizes their impact.

Recommendations of the Life Cycle Initiative

6. **Involve the LCA community globally in designing the approach, monitoring and evaluation, as well as in data collection and assessment of CE strategies:** The Life Cycle Initiative recommends involving the LCA community globally in the design, monitoring, and evaluation of circular economy strategies. This will help to ensure that circular economy strategies are based on sound

environmental principles, and that they are effectively implemented.

7. **Promote awareness and education on LCA and CE:** The Life Cycle Initiative recommends promoting awareness and education on LCA and circular economy. This will help to increase understanding of the importance of LCA and circular economy, and will help to promote the adoption of sustainable practices.

8. **Encourage collaboration between stakeholders:** The Life Cycle Initiative recommends encouraging collaboration between stakeholders in the development and implementation of circular economy strategies. This will help to ensure that circular economy strategies are based on a shared understanding of environmental principles, and that they are implemented in a way that maximizes their impact.

9. **Develop guidance documents and tools for LCA and CE:** The Life Cycle Initiative recommends developing guidance documents and tools for LCA and circular economy. This will help to ensure that businesses and organizations have access to the information and resources they need to effectively assess and implement circular economy strategies.

10. **Use case studies to demonstrate the benefits of LCA and CE:** The Life Cycle Initiative recommends using case studies to demonstrate the benefits of LCA and circular economy. This will help to showcase the potential of LCA and circular economy to improve sustainability and reduce waste and pollution.

Case studies of the Life Cycle Initiative's work include:

> ➤ The Global Guidance Principles for Life Cycle Assessment Databases, which provide guidance on best practices for developing and maintaining LCA databases. This work is aimed at improving the reliability and consistency of LCA data, which is critical for assessing CE strategies.

> ➤ The development of the Circularity Indicators Project, which aims to develop a comprehensive set of indicators to measure progress towards a circular economy. This project involves collaboration between the LCA community, industry, academia, and government stakeholders.

> ➤ The development of the Global Network of LCA Data Providers, which aims to facilitate collaboration and data sharing among LCA practitioners around the world. This network helps to improve the availability and quality of LCA data, which is critical for assessing CE strategies.

The Life Cycle Initiative provides valuable guidance, support, and collaboration opportunities for the LCA community as it works to assess and implement circular economy strategies. Through its work, the initiative can help to promote a more sustainable and circular economy that benefits both the environment and society.

09

Circularity Assessment Tool

The Circularity Assessment Too, developed by consortium (https://circitnord.com/) is an excel based tool which can be used to evaluate how circular your developed concepts are and how well the Guidelines for Circular Product Development have been implemented in the concepts. It is recommended that you have used or at least read through these guidelines before applying the tool.

With the Circularity Assessment Tool, you can evaluate your developed concepts based how well they fulfil important guidelines. The Circularity Potential Score for each of the guidelines depend on how important the individual guideline is and the level of fulfilment for the concepts. A high importance and low fulfilment is problematic and results in a high score (the lower the better). The Total Circularity Potential Score is the sum of the scores for each guideline and should be as low as possible. The tool can be used to compare different concepts and/or identify areas of improvement on the concept(s).

When to apply the tool?

The Circularity Assessment Tool should the used in the concept development phase, both for early product concepts and for concept selection before proceeding to the system level design phase.

This tool primarily targets those working on product design and development, such as designers, R&D professionals and product owners; however, it can support those working on sustainable development and the circular economy within the company. Although manufacturing companies are the main target, any private or public organization can also benefit from understanding and applying the mindset used to rethink the linear manufacturing process. The outline of the the tool and the incorporated guidelines takes it starting point from the motivation to think about sustainability and the importance of linking design and circularity.

The circularity assessment tool has been developed for use in the early product development process, i.e., planning and concept development to assess product designs and concepts in terms of circularity. The tool has been designed to calculate a "total circularity potential score" for at least two concepts so that they can be compared in terms of circularity. However, the circularity assessment tool can also be used for a single concept/product to identify hotspots and improvement potentials. It should be mentioned that circularity is not the only area in product design and development that is essential; hence, the full picture of product design and development, including other criteria such as cost, quality, delivery, and the market, needs to be considered. Therefore, this tool is an internal communication support for decision making in the early product development process.

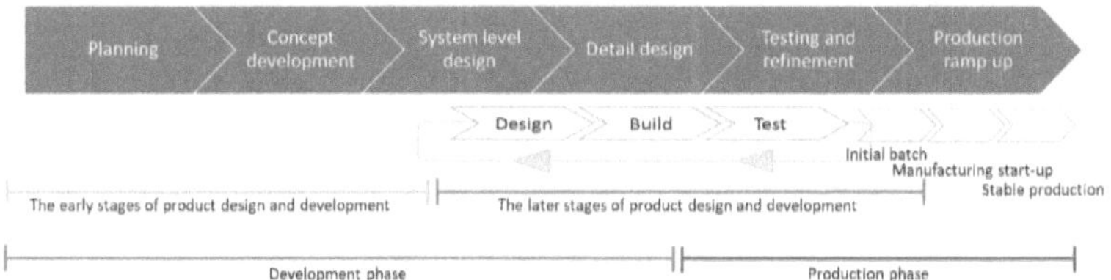

The tool presented here is based on guidelines and the circular strategy scanner developed in CIRCit project. Therefore, a short summary of circular strategy and general circular design guidelines are given in next tabs to refresh your memory.

Adopting circularity in product design and development by applying guidelines may positively and/or negatively affect other product design criteria, such as the intended functionalities, estimated product price and production cost, customer acceptance, technological requirements, ease of production, and the estimated development time and delivery dates. The ease of implementation of these circular guidelines also needs to be considered. The result provided by this tool is only an element in decision making, and it should be considered together with other product design and development criteria.

How to apply the tool:

Step 1: Preparation
You need to have (I) a good overview of the product lifecycle, possible environmental effects and the circularity aspects at each lifecycle stage, (II) a good understanding of the circular strategy scanner and different circular strategies, and (III) a good understanding of the design guidelines as a whole.

Step 2: Evaluate the concepts by indicating the "importance" and "level of fulfillment" for each design guideline

The circularity assessment tool calculates a "total circularity potential score" for at least two concepts. The lower the total circularity potential score is, the better the concept in terms of circularity. The total circularity potential score is calculated by multiplying two main criteria: "importance" and the "level of fulfillment". Each general design guideline is given a score under each criterion, for each one of the developed concepts. The scoring for each design guideline under each criterion is qualitative based on discussion among different stakeholders, including environmental managements/coordinators, product owners, product designers and developers, research and development professionals, manufacturing representatives, and marketing practitioners.

Indicate the "importance" and "level of fulfillment" for each design guideline

Step 2.1: Importance criterion refers to how important the general design guidelines are when designing and developing a specific product; this should be based on the previously selected circular strategies and the circularity goals determined. In this criterion, each general design guideline is given a score from 0 to 3

(3) really important
(2) moderately important
(1) slightly important
(0) not important.

The selection of scores is qualitative based on the product brief, the product development goals, the environmental and circularity goals, and previous experience from existing products on the market or previous generations. Agreement on importance should be achieved among all stakeholders involved, particularly manufacturing representatives, designers and marketing practitioners. Ensure consistency when comparing different product concepts by engaging the same group of people.

The level of importance is often the same for the concepts designed to deliver the same value and fulfill the same requirements, as they often follow the same goal with regard to the product development goal. However, in some cases, the level of importance might differ when a radical design is introduced and compared with other concepts.

Step 2.2: Level of fulfillment criterion refers to how much the general design guidelines are applied to/fulfilled for each one of the developed concepts. In this criterion, each general design guideline is given a score

(1) yes, the guideline has been completely fulfilled by this concept
(3) somehow but can be improved
(5) no, the guideline has not been fulfilled by this concept and it has to be

The selection of scores is qualitatively based on agreement among all stakeholders involved, particularly manufacturing representatives, designers and marketing practitioners.

Step 3: Calculate Circularity Potential Scores
On the basis of the data provided for each concept, the general design guidelines are given a score by multiplying "importance"

and the "level of fulfillment", resulting in a final score for each individual guideline:

(0): circularity is not a concern
(1, 2 or 3): does not require any changes in design and concept
(5 or 6): there are circularity improvement potentials in the current design and concept
(9 or 10): circularity improvements are necessary for the current design and concept
(15): vital and imperative design changes are necessary for circularity

Level of fulfillment

		1	3	5
Importnace	3	3	9	15
	2	2	6	10
	1	1	3	5
	0	0	0	0

15	Vital and imperative design changes are necessary for circularity
10 and 9	Circularity improvements are necessary for the current design and concept
6 and 5	There are circularity improvement potentials in the current design and concept
1-3	Does not require any changes in design and concept
	Circularity is not a concern

Step 4: Calculate the Total Circularity Potential Score for each concept

The total circularity potential score for each concept is then calculated by summing all the circularity potential scores of the individual guidelines. The lower the total circularity potential score is, the better the concept in terms of circularity.

Step 5: Visualization of results and interpretation

The results from tool can be interpreted in several steps.

Step 5.1: Identify circular hotspots and improvement potentials for each design concept

Look at the concepts individually and find which guidelines end up in the red and yellow areas. These are the areas that need to be revised and perhaps redesigned to include that specific circularity aspect/guideline. These aspects are vital and necessary for circularity and also for those strategies and goals you determined, while according to your own assessment, they have not been included in the current design. So you may want to start improving the design concepts based on these hotspots.

Step 5.2: Cross comparison of concepts in terms of circularity design guidelines

Now compare different concepts, which one has fewer hotspots? Which one has more? Which one is more consistent with your determined circularity goals and strategies? Which one is more cost effective to revise? Perhaps you would like to select the concept with more hotspots (red and yellow) and make a lot of changes? Or perhaps you directly go with the concept that ended up in green areas? These decisions need to be discussed in group to reach a consensus while considering other product development aspects. Document the discussion and the decision-making process for future reference.

Remember, even though the tool helps you to move towards circular economy and sustainability, the outcome will never be better than the quality of the input data collections and discussions. Therefore, try to collect as much relevant data as possible. If you have made a lot of rough estimations, the final result is not better than that!

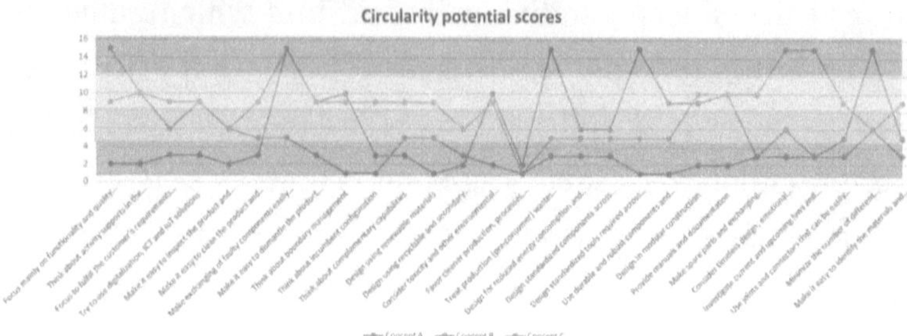

Circular Strategies

> **Rethink and reconfigure:** Changing business model innovation for circularity by rethinking the way of delivering the function and/or value proposition e.g. sharing economy, product service system, access-based sharing etc.

> **Reinvent:** Reinvent of current business through new meaning, complete dematerialization and radically different product and/or technology. Reinvent usually focuses on the use of digital technologies, particularly advances in information and communications technologies to provide a wide variety of services.

> **Raw materials and sourcing:** Changes in material sourcing to use more secondary, renewable and environmentally friendly materials

> **Manufacturing:** Changes in manufacturing technologies and equipment as well as production system to increase efficiency and effectiveness and have cleaner production

> **Product use and operation:** Changes in products to last longer and consume less consumables during the operation/use phase

> **Logistics and packaging:** Improving circularity, efficiency and effectiveness in logistics and also use more recyclable, renewable and environmentally friendly materials for packaging

> **Upgrade:** Add new changes and features to a functional product in order to extend the lifecycle and value beyond its original design condition

> **Repair and maintenance:** Correct, replace or fix faulty components of a defective product to return it to its original functionality to the same user to extend the lifespan of a product

> **Reuse:** Reuse of a (discarded) product that is still in good condition and fulfils its original function to keep the product functional and attractive to as many different users as possible, and for as long as possible, to extend and intensify the use of a product by preventing it from becoming obsolete

> **Refurbishment:** Repairing a returned product after a certain period of use to a satisfactory and acceptable mechanical specifications and operating condition by rebuilding or repairing major components that are close to failure, even when there are no reported or apparent faults in those components.

> **Remanufacture:** Disassembling, repairing, reassembling, testing and even upgrading a used product to look and perform with equivalent or higher performance and functionality

> **Repurpose:** Extending product lifecycle to new use cycles by using a product (discarded/not in use) or its parts for different functions

> **Recycle:** Any recovery operation by which wasted material is reprocessed into products, materials or substances whether for original or other purposes

> **Cascade:** Reusing materials with usually lower quality for a new application to extend resources timeline

> **Recover:** Energy recovering from incinerating materials with characteristics that no longer satisfy any application whatsoever

Circular Design Guidelines

> **Make it easy to inspect the product and components:** Easy and safe to inspect the product and components, particularly exchanging component. Use indications and manuals for testing and inspections

> **Make it easy to clean the product and components:** Avoid areas where dirt might collect like small holes, nooks, grooves sharp edges; remember that all components should be wear resistance and withstand the same chemicals and mechanical cleaning processes, liquid and chemicals, as well as temperatures, detergents and cleaning tools

> **Make exchanging of faulty components easily accessible:** Make disassembly points and components subject to break or fail easily accessible and preferably from one side

> **Make it easy to dismantle the product nondestructively:** Easy to open and dismount in a nondestructive way; using less glue and adhesives; robustness and wear resistance of joints; disassembly from one side; providing manuals

- **Think about boundary management:** Build and exploit cooperative networks, relationships and inter-organizational collaboration, focusing on the core business and strategy, and possibly merge and acquisitions

- **Think about incumbent configuration:** High level of autonomy and mobility, internal interpreter involvement, decentralization, and inter-functional collaboration combined with informal and organic organizational structures as well as having a look for long-term efficiency

- **Think about complementary capabilities:** Evaluating the chance of changing value proposition and become customer-oriented, along with access to distribution channels and leverage on specialized technologies

- **Design using renewable materials:** Reduce the use of materials which are limited in quantities such as tin, precious metals and use more renewable and bio-based materials if possible

- **Design using recyclable and secondary (recycled) materials:** Choose materials that have high recycling rate, and available recycling technology and market; increase materials compatibility that only one recycling method needed; increase the proportion of recycled material in your product and use less virgin raw materials

- **Consider toxicity and other environmental aspects of materials:** Use materials that that does not threatens biodiversity and do not contain hazardous chemicals; select materials that do not degenerate during the multiple lifecycles; select material with verified reliability; avoid materials which lose strength, get brittle or get discolored

➢ **Favor cleaner production, processes, machines and equipment:** Favor manufacturing processes, machines and equipment which use less energy and materials, generate less wastes and discharges less to air and water; select machines and equipment that require less frequent maintenance and cleaning and are with good working environment and ergonomic

➢ **Treat production (pre-consumer) wastes appropriately:** Think about type and amount of waste generated in manufacturing. What segment and fraction can those waste be separated to be able to facilitate pre-consumer recycling?

➢ **Design for reduced energy consumption and usage of renewable energy:** Design the product with reduced energy consumption, usage of renewable and clean energy; select production processes with high energy efficiency to reduced energy consumption; consider energy recovery of biological nutrients

➢ **Design standardized components across different products and models:** Compatibility and exchangeability of components required across other models and products e.g., same type and size of screws

➢ **Design standardized tools required across different products and models:** Compatibility and adaptability of tools required across other models and products e.g., same type and size of screwdriver

- **Use durable and robust components and materials:** Choose durable and robust component and material with a long lifespan; the lifespan of the different parts should be recognizable with indicators for wear; Avoid materials that might lose strength, get brittle or get discolored

- **Design in modular construction:** Divide product into different modules and put all the components that need to be exchanged or upgraded into one single module, thus lowering the effort

- **Provide manuals and documentation:** Provide user-friendly manuals and documentation on how to repair, upgrade etc. with signs on how to open the product and exchange components

- **Make spare parts and exchanging components easily available:** Exchanging components of products must be easy to find on the market and preferably be inexpensive

- **Consider timeless design, emotional attachment and compatibility:** Think about the effects that time and fashion will have on your product; simplicity, timeless design often and compatibility can be some ways to give product longevity, for example USB device

- **Investigate current and upcoming laws and regulations:** Comply with applicable laws and regulations like hazardous material or chemicals that now or later are harmful and might be banned

- **Use joints and connectors that can be easily opened and closed multiple times:** Generally, minimize the number of connectors and joints; use fastening devises which can be easily opened and closed multiple times; prioritize latch, snaps, clips and bolts and screws over welding, rivets, folding, staples, gluing which make a joint more difficult to demount

➢ **Minimize the number of different incompatible or dissimilar materials:** Minimize the number of different incompatible or dissimilar materials to facilitate shredding, regeneration and recycling; avoid molding and fusing incompatible materials; avoid multi-materials and composites

➢ **Make it easy to identify the materials and relevant information:** Create a system for identification of the individual components by for example RFID, barcode, tag or QR-code. Provide additional information about the product regarding material content, the material's age, number of times recycled, additives used, guide to component separation and process for the recycling.

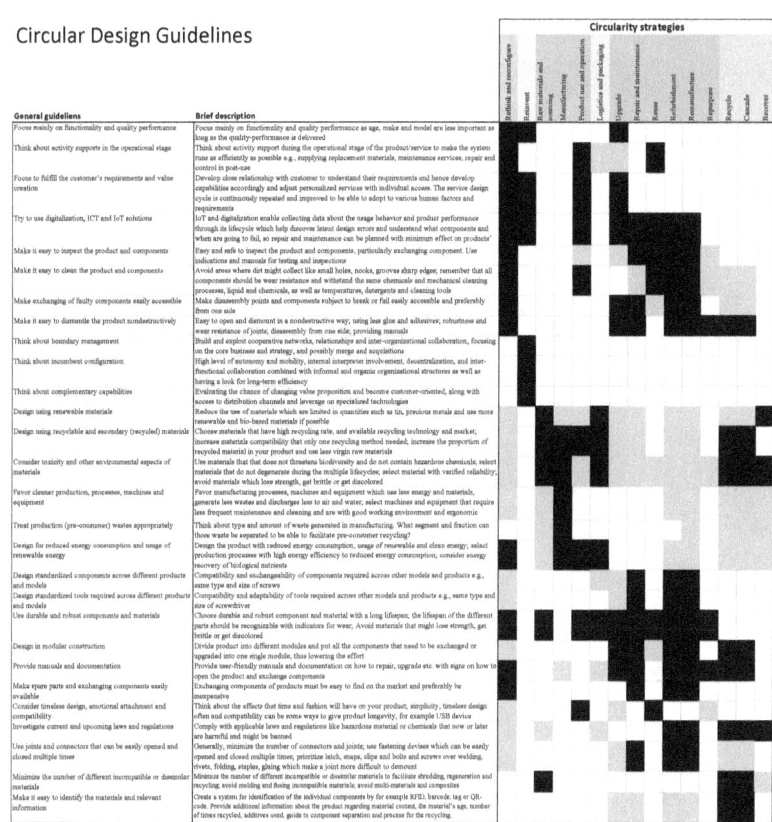

Circular Design Guidelines

Circularity strategies: Rethink and reconfigure · Reinvent · Raw materials and sourcing · Manufacturing · Product use and operation · Logistics and packaging · Upgrade · Repair and maintenance · Reuse · Refurbishment · Remanufacture · Repurpose · Recycle · Cascade · Recover

General guideliens	Brief description
Focus mainly on functionality and quality performance	Focus mainly on functionality and quality performance as age, make and model are less important as long as the quality-performance is delivered
Think about activity supports in the operational stage	Think about activity support during the operational stage of the product/service to make the system runs as efficiently as possible e.g., supplying replacement materials, maintenance services, repair and control in post-use
Focus to fulfill the customer's requirements and value creation	Develop close relationship with customer to understand their requirements and hence develop capabilities accordingly and adjust personalized services with individual access. The service design cycle is continuously repeated and improved to be able to adopt to various human factors and requirements
Try to use digitalization, ICT and IoT solutions	IoT and digitalization enable collecting data about the usage behavior and product performance through its lifecycle which help discover latent design errors and understand what components and when are going to fail, so repair and maintenance can be planned with minimum effect on products'
Make it easy to inspect the product and components	Easy and safe to inspect the product and components, particularly exchanging component. Use indications and manuals for testing and inspections
Make it easy to clean the product and components	Avoid areas where dirt might collect like small holes, nooks, grooves sharp edges; remember that all components should be wear resistance and withstand the same chemicals and mechanical cleaning processes, liquid and chemicals, as well as temperatures, detergents and cleaning tools
Make exchanging of faulty components easily accessible	Make disassembly points and components subject to break or fail easily accessible and preferably from one side
Make it easy to dismantle the product nondestructively	Easy to open and dismount in a nondestructive way; using less glue and adhesives, robustness and wear resistance of joints; disassembly from one side; providing manuals
Think about boundary management	Build and exploit cooperative networks, relationships and inter-organizational collaboration, focusing on the core business and strategy, and possibly merge and acquisitions
Think about incumbent configuration	High level of autonomy and mobility, internal interpreter involvement, decentralization, and inter-functional collaboration combined with informal and organic organizational structures as well as having a look for long-term efficiency
Think about complementary capabilities	Evaluating the chance of changing value proposition and become customer-oriented, along with access to distribution channels and leverage on specialized technologies
Design using renewable materials	Reduce the use of materials which are limited in quantities such as tin, precious metals and use more renewable and bio-based materials if possible
Design using recyclable and secondary (recycled) materials	Choose materials that have high recycling rate, and available recycling technology and market; increase materials compatibility that only one recycling method needed; increase the proportion of recycled material in your product and use less virgin raw materials
Consider toxicity and other environmental aspects of materials	Use materials that that does not threatens biodiversity and do not contain hazardous chemicals; select materials that do not degenerate during the multiple lifecycles; select material with verified reliability; avoid materials which lose strength, get brittle or get discolored
Favor cleaner production, processes, machines and equipment	Favor manufacturing processes, machines and equipment which use less energy and materials, generate less wastes and discharges less to air and water; select machines and equipment that require less frequent maintenance and cleaning and are with good working environment and ergonomic
Treat production (pre-consumer) wastes appropriately	Think about type and amount of waste generated in manufacturing. What segment and fraction can those waste be separated to be able to facilitate pre-consumer recycling?
Design for reduced energy consumption and usage of renewable energy	Design the product with reduced energy consumption, usage of renewable and clean energy; select production processes with high energy efficiency to reduced energy consumption; consider energy recovery of biological nutrients
Design standardized components across different products and models	Compatibility and exchangeability of components required across other models and products e.g., same type and size of screws
Design standardized tools required across different products and models	Compatibility and adaptability of tools required across other models and products e.g., same type and size of screwdriver
Use durable and robust components and materials	Choose durable and robust component and material with a long lifespan; the lifespan of the different parts should be recognizable with indicators for wear; Avoid materials that might lose strength, get brittle or get discolored
Design in modular construction	Divide product into different modules and put all the components that need to be exchanged or upgraded into one single module, thus lowering the effort
Provide manuals and documentation	Provide user-friendly manuals and documentation on how to repair, upgrade etc. with signs on how to open the product and exchange components
Make spare parts and exchanging components easily available	Exchanging components of products must be easy to find on the market and preferably be inexpensive
Consider timeless design, emotional attachment and compatibility	Think about the effects that time and fashion will have on your product; simplicity, timeless design often and compatibility can be some ways to give product longevity, for example USB device
Investigate current and upcoming laws and regulations	Comply with applicable laws and regulations like hazardous material or chemicals that now or later are harmful and might be banned
Use joints and connectors that can be easily opened and closed multiple times	Generally, minimize the number of connectors and joints; use fastening devises which can be easily opened and closed multiple times; prioritize latch, snaps, clips and bolts and screws over welding, rivets, folding, staples, gluing which make a joint more difficult to demount
Minimize the number of different incompatible or dissimilar materials	Minimize the number of different incompatible or dissimilar materials to facilitate shredding, regeneration and recycling; avoid molding and fusing incompatible materials; avoid multi-materials and composites
Make it easy to identify the materials and relevant information	Create a system for identification of the individual components by for example RFID, barcode, tag or QR-code. Provide additional information about the product regarding material content, the material's age, number of times recycled, additives used, guide to component separation and process for the recycling

The black cells indicate that the guideline has a direct effect on the circular strategy, while the grey cells indicate an indirect effect.

State your selected circularity goals:

General design guidelines	Importance to developing the product Really important (3) Moderately important (2) Slightly important (1) Not important (0)			Level of fulfillment (1) yes, the guideline has been completely fulfilled by this concept (3) somehow but can be improved (5) no, the guideline has not been fulfilled by this concept and it has to be			Circularity Potential Scores 15: Vital and imperative 10 and 9: Improvement are necessary 6 and 5: Potential circularity improvements 3, 2 and 1: No change required 0: Not a concern		
	Concept A	Concept B	Concept C	Concept A	Concept B	Concept C	Concept A	Concept B	Concept C
Focus mainly on functionality and quality performance	2	3	3	1	3	5	2	9	15
Think about activity supports in the operational stage	2	2	2	1	5	5	2	10	10
Focus to fulfill the customer's requirements and value creation	3	2	3	1	3	3	3	6	9
Try to use digitalization, ICT and IoT solutions	3	3	3	1	3	3	3	9	9
Make it easy to inspect the product and components	2	2	2	1	3	3	2	6	6
Make it easy to clean the product and components	3	1	3	1	5	3	3	5	9
Make exchanging of faulty components easily accessible	3	1	3	5	5	5	15	5	15
Make it easy to dismantle the product nondestructively	3	1	3	3	3	3	9	3	9
Think about boundary management	2	1	3	5	1	3	10	1	9
Think about incumbent configuration	3	1	3	1	1	3	3	1	9
Think about complementary capabilities	3	1	3	1	5	3	3	5	9
Design using renewable materials	1	1	3	1	5	3	1	5	9
Design using recyclable and secondary (recycled) materials	2	3	2	1	1	3	2	3	6
Consider toxicity and other environmental aspects of materials	2	2	3	5	1	3	10	2	9
Favor cleaner production, processes, machines and equipment	2	1	1	1	1	1	2	1	1
Treat production (pre-consumer) wastes appropriately	3	3	1	5	1	5	15	3	5
Design for reduced energy consumption and usage of renewable energy	2	3	1	3	1	5	6	3	5
Design standardized components across different products and models	2	3	1	3	1	5	6	3	5
Design standardized tools required across different products and models	3	1	1	5	1	5	15	1	5
Use durable and robust components and materials	3	1	1	3	1	5	9	1	5
Design in modular construction	3	2	2	3	1	5	9	2	10
Provide manuals and documentation	2	2	2	5	1	5	10	2	10
Make spare parts and exchanging components easily available	1	1	2	3	3	5	3	3	10
Consider timeless design, emotional attachment and compatibility	1	2	3	3	3	5	3	6	15
Investigate current and upcoming laws and regulations	1	1	3	3	3	5	3	3	15
Use joints and connectors that can be easily opened and closed multiple times	1	3	3	5	1	3	5	3	9
Minimize the number of different incompatible or dissimilar materials	3	2	2	5	3	3	15	6	6
Make it easy to identify the materials and relevant information	1	3	3	5	1	3	5	3	9
Total Circularity potential Score with inclusion of the effect (the smaller the better)							174	110	243

Concept B is more circular

Bottle example

State your selected circularity goals:

General design guidelines	Improtance to developing the product Really important (3) Moderately important (2) Slightly important (1) Not important (0)			Level of fulfillment (1) yes, the guideline has been completely fulfilled by this concept (3) somehow but can be improved (5) no, the guideline has not been fulfilled by this concept and it has to be			Circularity Potential Scores 15: Vital and imperative 10 and 9: Improvement are necessary 6 and 5: Potential circularity improvements 3, 2 and 1: No change required 0: Not a concern		
	Concept A	Concept B	Concept C	Concept A	Concept B	Concept C	Concept A	Concept B	Concept C
Focus mainly on functionality and quality performance	2	3	3	1	3	5	2	9	15
Think about activity supports in the operational stage	2	2	2	1	5	5	2	10	10
Focus to fulfill the customer's requirements and value creation	3	2	3	1	3	3	3	6	9
Try to use digitalization, ICT and IoT solutions	3	3	3	1	3	3	3	9	9
Make it easy to inspect the product and components	2	2	2	1	3	3	2	6	6
Make it easy to clean the product and components	3	1	3	1	5	3	3	5	9
Make exchanging of faulty components easily accessible	3	1	3	5	5	5	15	5	15
Make it easy to dismantle the product nondestructively	3	1	3	3	3	3	9	3	9
Think about boundary management	2	1	3	5	1	3	10	1	9
Think about incumbent configuration	3	1	3	1	1	3	3	1	9
Think about complementary capabilities	3	1	3	1	5	3	3	5	9
Design using renewable materials	1	1	3	1	5	3	1	5	9
Design using recyclable and secondary (recycled) materials	2	3	2	1	1	3	2	3	6
Consider toxicity and other environmental aspects of materials	2	2	3	5	1	3	10	2	9
Favor cleaner production, processes, machines and equipment	2	1	1	1	1	1	2	1	1
Treat production (pre-consumer) wastes appropriately	3	3	1	5	1	5	15	3	5
Design for reduced energy consumption and usage of renewable energy	2	3	1	3	1	5	6	3	5
Design standardized components across different products and models	2	3	1	3	1	5	6	3	5
Design standardized tools required across different products and models	3	1	1	5	1	5	15	1	5
Use durable and robust components and materials	3	1	1	3	1	5	9	1	5
Design in modular construction	3	2	2	3	1	5	9	2	10
Provide manuals and documentation	2	2	2	5	1	5	10	2	10
Make spare parts and exchanging components easily available	1	1	2	3	3	5	3	3	10
Consider timeless design, emotional attachment and compatibility	1	2	3	3	3	5	3	6	15
Investigate current and upcoming laws and regulations	1	1	3	3	3	5	3	3	15
Use joints and connectors that can be easily opened and closed multiple times	1	3	3	5	1	3	5	3	9
Minimize the number of different incompatible or dissimilar materials	3	2	2	5	3	3	15	6	6
Make it easy to identify the materials and relevant information	1	3	3	5	1	3	5	3	9
Total Circularity potential Score with inclusion of the effect (the smaller the better)							174	110	243

Concept B is more circular

Graphs and visualization

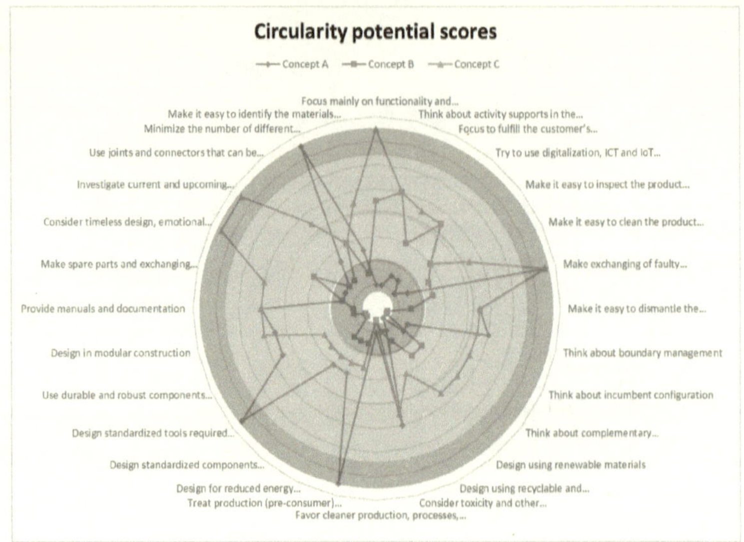

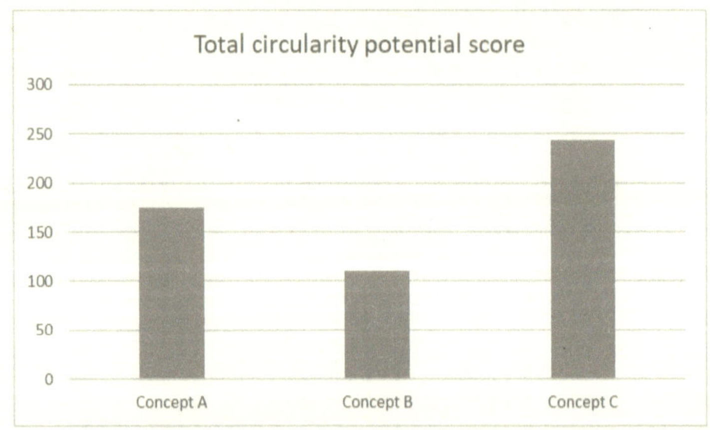

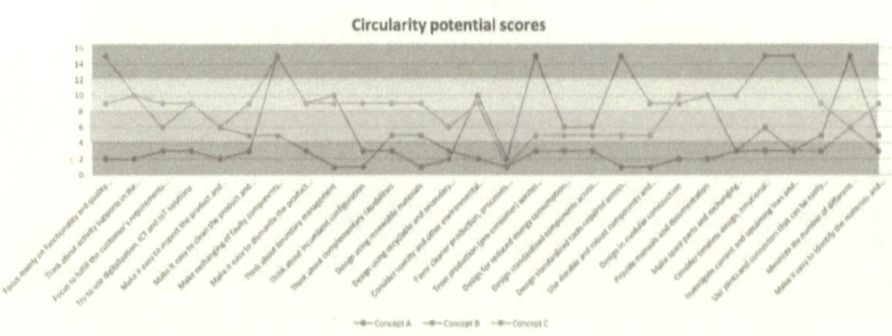

10

Circularity Assessment Tool

As we draw the final chapter of our journey through the intersection of the circular economy and digital transformation, it is fitting to reflect upon the key points we've explored and to gaze into the future, where these transformative concepts promise to reshape industries, societies, and the planet.

Summary of Key Points

Throughout this book, we have embarked on a comprehensive exploration of the circular economy and its symbiotic relationship with digital transformation. Here is a recap of the key takeaways:

The Circular Economy (Chapter II):

- We have discovered that the circular economy is not just an environmental endeavor but a holistic approach to transforming industries and economies.
- A series of case studies has exemplified the diverse range of industries and organizations successfully

implementing circular economy practices, reaping both ecological and economic rewards.

➤ We have acknowledged that the transition to a circular economy is not without its challenges, from shifting business models to altering consumer behaviors. However, understanding and addressing these challenges are critical for success.

➤ The vital connection between the circular economy and the United Nations Sustainable Development Goals (UN SDGs) was unveiled, emphasizing its potential to drive global sustainability.

Digital Transformation (Chapter III):

➤ We have established that digital transformation is an essential enabler for the circular economy, fostering innovation, efficiency, and connectivity across industries.

➤ A gallery of case studies from various sectors has demonstrated how digital technologies can bring about significant improvements in productivity, customer experiences, and sustainability.

➤ Yet, we have recognized that implementing digital transformation is not a simple task, with challenges related to data security, technology adoption, and change management requiring careful consideration.

Intersection of Circular Economy and Digital Transformation (Chapter IV):

➤ We have explored the opportunities presented by digital technologies to accelerate the circular economy, such as tracking and tracing materials, enhancing resource management, and creating circular supply chains.

➤ Real-world examples have showcased how digital transformation augments circular business models, generating greater resource efficiency and reducing waste.

➤ However, we have also acknowledged the challenges faced in harnessing digital technology for circularity, including the need for investment, digital literacy, and interoperability.

Building the Circular Economy with Digital Transformation (Chapter VI):

➤ We have outlined practical steps to guide organizations in implementing circular business models using digital technologies, emphasizing the importance of strategy, collaboration, and continuous improvement.

➤ Through case studies, we have witnessed how successful circular economy models have been constructed with digital transformation at their core.

➤ The role of government policies and regulations in accelerating the circular economy was explored, illustrating how legislative support can drive the adoption of circular practices.

Challenges and Solutions (Chapter VII):

➤ We have identified common challenges faced in the implementation of circular economy models enhanced by digital transformation, including resistance to change, lack of standardization, and data privacy concerns.

> Solutions have been proposed to overcome these challenges, ranging from employee training and engagement to industry collaboration and technological innovations.

Relation Between Circular Economics and Life Cycle Assessment (Chapter VIII):

> We have recognized the strength of Life Cycle Assessment (LCA) as a valuable tool for assessing the environmental and economic impacts of circular economy strategies.

> Challenges in applying LCA to circular economy practices were acknowledged, with emphasis on the need for expanded data availability and methodological development.

> Advantages and recommendations from the Life Cycle Initiative have been presented alongside relevant case studies, underlining the potential of LCA to inform and guide circularity assessment.

With these insights in mind, we stand at the crossroads of a significant transformation in the way we design, produce, consume, and manage resources.

Future Outlook for the Intersection of Circular Economy and Digital Transformation

The future holds boundless potential for the circular economy and digital transformation. Here are some key areas where we anticipate exciting developments:

1. **Technological Advancements**: As digital technologies continue to evolve, we can expect breakthroughs in IoT, AI, blockchain, and data analytics, further optimizing resource use and enabling more circular business models.

2. **Cross-Industry Synergy**: Industries and sectors will increasingly collaborate to create interconnected circular supply chains and ecosystems, promoting resource sharing and reducing waste.

3. **Global Adoption**: With the increasing awareness of environmental challenges, we anticipate more governments and organizations worldwide to embrace the circular economy and digital transformation as core strategies for a sustainable future.

4. **Consumer Empowerment**: Digital technologies will empower consumers to make more informed and sustainable choices, fostering a culture of reusing, sharing, and recycling.

5. **Policy and Regulation**: Governments will play an essential role in shaping the landscape, with regulations and incentives driving circular practices and responsible digital transformation.

6. **Research and Innovation**: The intersection of circularity and digitalization will continue to be a fertile ground for research, development, and innovation, leading to new tools, standards, and best practices.

Our journey through the intersection of the circular economy and digital transformation may be concluding, but it marks the beginning of an era where sustainability, efficiency, and innovation harmonize in ways that have the potential to reshape our world for the better. As we look to this future, we encourage readers to stay curious, adapt to change, and be agents of positive transformation in their respective fields. Together, we can accelerate the transition to a circular, digitalized future, where sustainability and economic prosperity walk hand in hand.

Thank you for joining me on this enlightening journey, and may your endeavors in the world of circular economy and digital transformation be fruitful and impactful.

About the Author

Vijay Karna has over two decades of experience with expertise in business transformation & digitalization to blend industry domain flavor and ensure optimal alignment to client business needs along with providing a differentiated solution to the client.

Vijay is a Decision Analyst, has experience in assessing clients on digital readiness on Business Models, Product & Service Portfolio, Market & Customer Access, Value Chains & Processes, IT Architecture, Compliance, Organization & Culture change.

Vijay is leading transformation projects on emerging technologies like automation, Industrial Internet of Things (IIoT), Sustainability Assessment, LCA Assessment, Circular Economy Assessment & implementation etc. Vijay worked on SMART Enterprise Asset Management including Operational Technologies (OT) – Engineering Technologies (ET) – Information Technologies (IT) integration. He has experience in ERP Account, Program, Project Management, Application Design & Development, Solution Management and Practice Building; successfully set up CoE& PMO.

His prime focus is on leveraging increasing employee adoption and usage for change initiatives that would happen as an outcome of transformation programs, projects and change initiatives towards delivering maximum business value and profitability.

He has PhD in IT Operations Management (IT-OT integration) & how to reduce human intervention in IT management. He developed a tool on Business Process Impact & Readiness Assessment which enhances the efficiency & acceptability of transformation programs including automation.

Vijay is certified Sustainability Reporting practitioner.

Vijay is Author of the book 'Managing Organizational Business Process Change' & Co Author of Book on 'Integrated Framework using SOA for Oil & Gas Companies'.